Praise for *A Leader's Guide to Giving a Memorable Speech*

"Dr. Palmisano's book is of supreme importance to all. An indispensable template to educate all who wish to write or give speeches. A buoy for support of all who have shuddered in anxiety before giving an occasional address. A beacon of hope for audiences that they will cease being subjected to boring, ill-prepared, and irrelevant speeches."

—Ronald J. French, MD, reigned as Rex,
King of New Orleans Mardi Gras in 2007

"A surgeon, an attorney, an extraordinary leader, an author, and a man fully engaged in the richness of life, Dr. Palmisano, the bestselling author of *On Leadership*, has written another remarkable book. *A Leader's Guide to Giving a Memorable Speech* delivers on the promise of the title with an abundance of practical advice that you will find useful whether you are an experienced public speaker or deathly afraid of addressing an audience. But the book offers much more. You will learn how to envision your message, shape it, and deliver it beautifully, as Dr. Palmisano interweaves his own vast experience with that of great writers and orators throughout history. It is impossible to read this book without wanting to highlight it, and you will find yourself making notes for your next speech. You will enjoy every page for the richness of the writing, the curated tour of literature and oratory, and the no-nonsense wisdom presented. You will learn how to achieve memorable communication in contexts ranging from an elevator pitch to a TED talk. You will see words that have moved the wheel of history and explore literary devices that have been effective for thousands of years. You not only need this book, you will enjoy it immensely."

—Richard E. Anderson, MD, FACP, Chairman and CEO
of The Doctors Company

"'If there is an awful malady in the world, it is stage fright,' Mark Twain recalled. 'My knees were shaking . . . I didn't know whether I could stand.' I felt those sensations at age seven giving a camp lecture. Dr. Palmisano's book would have saved me. Built on the remarkable experiences of a superb speaker whose own memorable addresses I've heard, Dr. Palmisano assembles principles from history and literature to create a spinal column of rhetorical devices, demeanor, and inside knowledge that can structure and polish in-person or media success for first-timers or the experienced. Twain would have loved it like me."

—Mark B. Constantian, MD, FACS, Traveling Professor, American Society for Aesthetic Plastic Surgery

"In this easy-to-read, practical, and well-organized guide to public speaking, Donald Palmisano, MD, notes the importance of 'being yourself.' He personifies this advice consistently and brilliantly—in person, in print, on stage, on TV and radio, and in this book, providing invaluable tools for more effective communication and success."

—Donna Baver Rovito, editor, *Physician Family Magazine*

"Dr. Palmisano's leadership and public speaking seminar is highly rated by our medical students due to his uncanny ability to convey important lessons through storytelling. This book will undoubtedly provide much-needed practical strategies for becoming an effective, engaging, and memorable speaker."

—Jennifer W. Gibson, PhD, director, Office of Medical Education at Tulane University School of Medicine

"When I was offered the chance to have a look at *A Leader's Guide to Giving a Memorable Speech* by Dr. Donald Palmisano, I jumped at the chance. Tulane medical students have had the opportunity to take his elective course, 'Leadership: How to Give a Memorable Speech.' Well, I missed my chance by only forty-five years or so I thought. Now, we all have that second chance for leadership guru Dr. Palmisano has synthesized this course into this, his latest book. Drawing from seemingly boundless examples from Demosthenes to Mick Jagger, from Shakespeare to Lou Gehrig, this book comes fully loaded with practical tips, examples, and directions enough to make Mark Twain take notes. This book is also chock full of the lagniappe of his own life experience. From the young boy frozen with stage fright to 'Aloha, Mahalo' in his farewell address to the Louisiana State Medical Society, Dr. Palmisano pulls the reader alongside him as he revisits the highway of his life while sharing the insights gained at every rest stop on the path to leadership. Whether tasked with addressing your local PTA or your state legislature, you need to look no further than *A Leader's Guide to Giving a Memorable Speech* for inspiration. This is truly the only how-to guide you will ever need. I wish I had seen this book before giving my own inaugural address."

—Art Fougner, MD, president of the Medical Society
State of New York 2019–2020

"Giving a high-impact speech requires a thorough understanding of the art and science of passionate communication, and in *A Leader's Guide to Giving a Memorable Speech*, Dr. Don Palmisano has drawn from over two thousand years of wisdom and structure to put all the keys in your hands. As important and immediately useful to a speaker as a six-gun was to a lawman in the old west. Highly readable, immediately useful, and deeply enjoyable!"

—John J. Nance, Aviation Analyst for *ABC World News*,
author, and speaker

"Storytelling at its best! Dr. Donald Palmisano takes you from Aristotle and Cicero to modern day orators, with insights on avoiding panic and other pitfalls, the use of rhetorical devices, and how to wow audiences from this masterful speaker who has done over one thousand speeches and interviews."

—John N. Kennedy, United States Senator, Louisiana

"Speaking powerfully, with confidence, can transform your career. Palmisano, himself a famed speaker, provides tips and techniques that are invaluable."

—Philip K. Howard, bestselling author of *The Death of Common Sense* and leader in legal reform

A LEADER'S GUIDE TO GIVING A MEMORABLE SPEECH

How to Deliver a Message and Captivate an Audience

Donald J. Palmisano, MD, JD, FACS
Foreword by Tess Gerritsen

Skyhorse Publishing

Skyhorse Publishing books may be purchased in bulk at special discounts for sales promotion, corporate gifts, fund-raising, or educational purposes. Special editions can also be created to specifications. For details, contact the Special Sales Department, Skyhorse Publishing, 307 West 36th Street, 11th Floor, New York, NY 10018 or info@skyhorsepublishing.com.

Skyhorse® and Skyhorse Publishing® are registered trademarks of Skyhorse Publishing, Inc.®, a Delaware corporation.

Visit our website at www.skyhorsepublishing.com.

10 9 8 7 6 5 4 3 2 1

Library of Congress Cataloging-in-Publication Data is available on file.

Cover design by Daniel Brount
Cover photo credit: Getty Images

Print ISBN: 978-1-5107-5527-7
Ebook ISBN: 978-1-5107-5535-2

Printed in the United States of America.

TABLE OF CONTENTS

DEDICATION

To my loving wife, Robin, my muse, advisor, confidante, in-house editor, and defender; a kind and generous lady who makes my dreams come true and brings joy to my life.

FOREWORD
BY TESS GERRITSEN

Many of us know the symptoms: the racing heart, the sweaty palms, and shaky hands that come with having to give a speech. *Glossophobia*, or fear of public speaking, is so common that up to half of the population avoids any situation that requires addressing a public forum. Yet for many of us, public speaking is a skill essential to our success at school, at work, or as a participating member of our communities. Whether it's presenting a report in class or in the boardroom, whether it's speaking to a television camera or at a town meeting, most of us, at some time in our lives, will need to face our fears and speak before an audience.

And that's where this book comes in.

Dr. Donald Palmisano is one of the most gifted speakers I've ever had the pleasure of meeting, and in *A Leader's Guide to Giving a Memorable Speech* he shares the lessons he's learned from decades of experience giving speeches. He explores a speaker's worst nightmares: the panic when your mind goes blank and you can't think of a thing to say, or when your projector dies, taking down your slideshow. How do you recover from these disasters?

In this guide, you'll learn how to deal with the unexpected mishaps that can beset any speaker, from lost slides to missing notes. You'll learn how to create a bond with your audience, emotionally investing them with what you're about to say. Using as examples powerful speeches delivered by historical icons, from Queen Elizabeth I to Martin Luther King Jr., Dr. Palmisano reveals the rhetorical tricks of the trade: the dramatic pause, the art of repetition, and the power of metaphor and dynamic writing. You'll also learn how important it is to include stories in your speech. Long after the speech has ended, what your audience will remember are the stories you told or the anecdote that moved them. And for those who must speak on-camera, there are tips for you too, with advice about makeup and wardrobe, how to prep for remote recordings, and what to expect in a television studio.

I wish I'd had this guidebook thirty years ago, when I started my career as an author and speaker. Instead I had to learn the hard way, my heart pounding as I stood before countless audiences. I muddled my way through painful television interviews, grew flustered when my slides were displayed upside down, and discovered what it feels like when the energy in a room suddenly collapses. Eventually I did learn the tricks of giving a great speech, but I had to suffer through years of trial and error and countless mistakes.

This guide can save you from that pain.

—Tess Gerritsen,
New York Times bestselling author

INTRODUCTION

WHY ANOTHER BOOK ON SPEECHES?

In an orator, the acuteness of the logicians, the wisdom of the philosophers, the language almost of poetry, the memory of lawyers, the voice of tragedians, the gesture almost of the best actors, is required. Nothing therefore is more rarely found among mankind than a consummate orator.

— Cicero

Why another book on speeches? Search the Internet and you will get a potpourri of seemingly endless books on the subject. There are books that list speeches that the authors think are great. There are books offering advice on how to write a speech. There are books on how to deliver a speech. It can be overwhelming.

Consider this: If you had to pick someone as a bodyguard to accompany you through a war zone, would you pick someone who writes about safety precautions in wartime, but has never been in a war zone? Or would you pick someone who fought in wars on the front lines and also behind enemy lines?

My point? Experience counts! Experience combined with the success of an author makes the choice easy. With every book on speeches, consider how many speeches the author has delivered successfully,

My method of writing and delivering speeches is backed up by over a thousand speeches and media interviews with local, national, and international newspapers, magazines, television, radio, and Internet postings. My experience includes debates with powerful adversaries before large audiences and even on national TV, as well as testifying many times before Congress and in multiple state legislatures.

On July 9, 2003, I spoke at the National Press Club as the National Press Club Newsmaker. *Vital Speeches of the Day* and *Executive Speeches* magazines have published my speeches.[1-7] Most importantly, the audiences' written responses and standing ovations to my speeches demonstrate a winning technique.*

This book grew out of a popular elective course I created and teach to third- and fourth-year medical students at Tulane University School of Medicine titled, "Leadership: How to Give a Memorable Speech." I share with the students the advice and techniques of master speakers and writers from over the centuries that are available to all of us. In this book, I compile those treasures and explain the art of storytelling, rhetorical devices, memory aids, and how to avoid the potholes of speech composition and delivery.

You do not need to read the chapters of this book in the order presented. Read them all as a means of developing an expertise

---

* Sample audience comments:

"I have never heard such sustained applause in my thirty-eight years of attending—and, boy, did you deserve it!"

"Excellent. His enthusiasm is remarkable."

"Outstanding, entertaining, knowledgeable, superb."

"Your speeches were different, new, thoughtful, passionate, and inspiring!"

"You were great tonight on Hardball. You are an excellent debater."

"I saw you this morning on Fox News with Tony Snow and you did an excellent job."

"I enjoyed the meeting last weekend. I was so impressed with Donald Palmisano. He is a better public speaker than most if not all of the people in Congress and the White House. What a dynamo."

Example of sustained standing ovation, *Dr. Palmisano's farewell speech to the AMA*: https://donaldpalmisano.com.

in speech writing and delivery, but don't hesitate to go directly to any chapter that helps with an issue you find worrisome at the moment.

This book is essential for executives, but will be useful for a wide audience because everyone is a potential speaker. Invitations are not needed to post a speech on the Internet, on YouTube, or on some future hi-tech transmission of video and audio that could be watched by millions. Perhaps a hologram projected to faraway places with strange sounding names!

I especially hope to reach younger individuals in their formative years with the lessons contained in this book. The earlier a skill is learned and the longer it is practiced, the more the skill becomes ingrained. Prepare your kids and other youngsters for college and beyond with the speech writing and delivery guidance in this book. The need for proper appearance and editing software are emphasized if readers aspire to vlog as their entry into the speech arena.

The words of Cicero from over two thousand years ago remain true today, and this book will reveal the secrets to memorable speeches so you can aspire to Cicero's standard of public speaking. The lessons learned from studying this book will relieve your anxiety in presenting, whether you are an executive talking at a national conference; a student giving a speech in class; or a graduate interviewing for a job. This book will give you the skill set needed for composing and delivering a speech that will delight your audience and have them embrace and recall your message for years to come.

Now let's go on a journey to overcome the fear of public speaking; to learn the magic of personal stories and rhetorical devices; and to study lessons from speeches of the past, some hundreds and thousands of years ago. Read, learn, and speak your way to success! Let the adventure begin!

Chapter 1

PANIC!

Fear is the mind-killer.

—Frank Herbert, *Dune*

Thirty-five years ago, I sat in a large auditorium with five hundred people in mid-America waiting to give my first national-audience speech. My presentation would follow the keynote speaker who now walked onto the stage. He was trim, well groomed, and dressed in an expensive Italian suit, perhaps a multi-thousand-dollar Brioni[1] or Armani[2].

The lights dimmed and a spotlight highlighted him. He looked like he had just stepped off the cover of *GQ* magazine. I took out my pen and notepad, assuming I could learn a lot from him. The middle aisle was five seats from me and a device on a cart was rolled adjacent to our row of seats. It was larger than a regular 35mm projector.

The speaker paused dramatically, looking to the right and then to the left. He then pointed at the device in the middle aisle near me. A cloud came out of the top. In my naive state, and because I had just read an article about holograms, I concluded a hologram was about to drift across the audience. I thought, "Wow, take good notes! What a showman!"

Unfortunately, it was not a high-tech hologram. It was a large projector on fire! The auditorium staff quickly put out the fire before everyone bolted out of the auditorium. Meanwhile, the keynote speaker just stood on the stage and stared at the audience. The dramatic pause had turned into a panic freeze. The audience stared back. About two minutes later, someone tapped me on the back and said, "Dr. Palmisano, please go to the stage and do your speech now."

The keynote speaker was removed from the stage by two people and I never heard his speech nor heard of him again. Now *that* is a memorable keynote presentation, but not the kind that wins applause. The speaker planned to rely on the slides in that projector and had no backup notes.

Under-preparation and panic are not uncommon among public speakers and performers. Picture this scene:

An eight-year-old boy enters the stage of his boarding school to say the opening line of the school's Christmas play. He was new to the school and anxious to make a positive impression. He had practiced his line over and over during school recess and in the dark hours of night before sleep overcame him: "And Joseph also went up from Galilee, out of the city of Nazareth, into Judaea, unto the City of David, which is called Bethlehem." As he planted his feet on stage where the play director instructed, he spotted his parents in the audience. He took a deep breath and began to speak when an unrehearsed spotlight came on and blinded him, causing the audience to disappear and his memory to fail. Try as he might, he could not recall the Biblical quote he had painstakingly committed to memory. He had taken no notes on stage to which he might refer, but he spotted a boy from class with whom he had practiced. "Tell me the first word," he pleaded with his new friend, but his friend replied, "What?" and stared back at him. As he stood for what felt for hours staring into the bright light unable to utter a word, a Christian Brother walked onto the stage to remove him. That panicked, embarrassed eight-year-old boy was me, and it is a life lesson I will never forget.

This book was written, in part, to ensure that these disasters do not happen to you. Fear stalks first-time speakers, and even most seasoned speakers will admit to feeling an involuntary adrenaline rush as they step to the podium.

Some speakers go into a stall, as in aircraft lingo—spiral to the ground, crash, and burn. My flight instructor taught me to not panic if a stall and spin occur. Inexperienced pilots tend to pull the nose of the plane up in that crisis, which will cause the wings to lose lift and the plane to spiral to the ground. Pilots are taught to keep cool, put the nose of the plane down, and give opposite rudder to the spin so that the plane levels out. The same is true with public speaking: don't panic, keep cool, look at your notes, take a deep breath, and begin!

Computers and projectors can fail. Your mind can go blank. Any number of circumstances can threaten the execution of your speech as you planned it. But the key to success in delivering a memorable speech in a positive manner is to be armed with a back-up plan in anticipation of such impediments.

I call it the "Big A" in my "Big A and 25 C's of Risk Management" lecture.[3] The "Big A" stands for anticipating what could go wrong and being prepared. Simply stated, to ensure you enchant your audience with your spoken word you always should have an alternative way to see your speech notes, even when you think you know them by heart. When you have a copy of your speech or key words of each section of the speech with you on the podium, a glance at the notes reboots your mind and allays your anxiety. The same solution applies if your audio-visual supports fail.

Practice is another means of reducing anxiety and minimizing the likelihood of panic as you step before an audience to speak. Reflect on the life of Demosthenes of Greece, who was born in 384 BC. He learned rhetoric to go to court to recover money from guardians who mishandled his inheritance after his father's death. In addition to the burdens of the legal challenge in court, Plutarch wrote that Demosthenes had "an inarticulate and stammering pronunciation" that he overcame by practicing speaking with pebbles in his mouth. Demosthenes also practiced his speeches repeatedly. While the pebbles are not necessarily beneficial, the practice certainly is helpful.

Benjamin Franklin famously stated, "Practice makes perfect." Whether or not perfection is guaranteed from practice, I do think it is indisputable that practice helps to reduce fear of public speaking. The more familiar you are with the task at hand, the less apprehensive you will be. While various methods of practicing speech delivery will be discussed intermittently in this book, my first experience in speech practice methodology came from my father, New Orleans Police Major Dominic Palmisano.

Even today I see in my mind that scene of forgetting my line in my first Christmas play at my new boarding school. My parents were in the audience and I still recall how concerned I was that I had embarrassed them. I apologized when my parents found me after the play and my Dad put his arm around me and said, "Don't worry, son. The next time I see you I will bring you something to practice speaking and what happened tonight will never happen again."

When Dad came to visit six weeks later, he gave me an Ekotape reel-to-reel tape recorder.[4]

Dad showed me how to work the rather large device and told me, "Practice speaking into the tape recorder fifteen minutes every day after school and the problem you had at the Christmas play will never happen again." I did as Dad instructed. For fifteen minutes every day, I spoke aloud poetry, passages from books, and even random thoughts into the tape recorder. I listened to my voice. I grew more and more confident of my speaking ability, and that paralyzing panic never happened again throughout my years in school and during decades of public speaking.

Lessons Learned

- Panic can occur at the start of a speech or later with the mind going blank, especially if a mishap occurs such as projection slide failure.
- The risk management solution to prevent the panic when the mind goes blank is to always have a copy of your speech on the podium.
- Practice, practice, and practice your speech to allay anxiety in public speaking.

Chapter 2

THE FOUR KEY ELEMENTS OF A MEMORABLE SPEECH

Somewhere there is a map of how it can be done.
—Ben Stein

Fear of public speaking is common. It can paralyze your mind when you look at the audience. You can't remember the first word. Your heart races. Sweat drips. The audience stares. Seconds seem like minutes.

Too many smart people are hesitant to take leadership roles because of a fear of public speaking. What to do? Here is what I found to be effective for a memorable speech after completing over a thousand speeches and interviews worldwide. I teach leadership and public speaking and know my technique to be effective with students and executives. Master these four key elements of a memorable speech as your foundation to speech writing and delivery with eloquence.

Four Key Elements of a Memorable Speech

1. Knowledge of topic
2. Passion
3. Presentation skill
4. Stories

Knowledge of Topic

You must supply both the knowledge of the topic and the passion. This chapter will focus on the third and fourth elements: presentation skill and stories. However, let's discuss knowledge of the topic and passion briefly.

You display your knowledge of the topic when you speak and engage in questions from the audience. Knowledge distinguishes the actor who is reading a script from a true expert who has knowledge from study and experience. You may have experienced some politicians who read from a teleprompter and then rush off the stage stating that other obligations do not permit time for them to answer questions. Or you may have heard an elected official give a summary of the law that is obviously incorrect to knowledgeable listeners. Displaying a lack of knowledge or stating incorrect facts destroys the credibility of the speaker. These individuals usually are presenting speeches written by others and knowledge of the details and true passion are lacking.

Passion

Passion when delivering a speech energizes the audience. The monotone low volume speaker is a sure-fire sleep inducer.

Passion combined with knowledge and skill in presentation can cast a magical spell on the audience. Think of memorable scenes in movies that exhibit great passion: where the protagonist rallies the troops, stops a mob with fiery words, or delivers a logical argument in a trial laced with poetic phrases that would please Shakespeare. In Chapter 14, I give examples of passionate and persuasive speech, including the text of the powerful real-life closing argument of the chief American prosecutor in the Nazi trials at Nuremberg at the end of World War II.

Think of Robin Williams in *Good Will Hunting*:

And you wouldn't know what it's like to be her angel and to have that love for her to be there forever. Through anything. Through cancer. You wouldn't know about sleeping sitting up in a hospital room for two months holding her hand because the doctors could see in your eyes that the term "visiting hours" don't apply to you. You don't know about real loss, because that only occurs when you love something more than you love yourself. I doubt you've ever dared to love anybody that much. I look at you; I don't see an intelligent, confident man; I see a cocky, scared shitless kid. But you're a genius, Will. No one denies that. No one could possibly understand the depths of you. But you presume to know everything . . .

See also the scene from *Rocky Balboa* in which actor Sylvester Stallone explains to his son the importance of not being a social metaphysician, that is, letting others' opinions of you control you.[1]

When a speaker is passionate, the audience concludes that they are seeing an authentic person, not an actor. A short article, *Why is Passion Important in Public Speaking* by Nick Morgan in *Forbes* online December 23, 2014, points out that passion is essential to communicate to the audience. He believes passion allows the audience to take measure of the speaker's values.[2]

Presentation Skill

First, let's memorize an acronym I developed as an organizational tool for skilled presentation:

CODAC
Not spelled as the film company "Kodak," but **C-O-D-A-C**. **CODAC** stands for **C**ontent, **O**rganization, **D**elivery, **A**ction, **C**ontrol.

CODAC gives you a template for developing a memorable speech. If you write **CODAC** on a piece of paper you take with you on stage and list key words of your speech next to each initial, it can be used as a memory aid if your mind goes blank when the spotlight hits your face as you step to the podium.

C is for content. This can include the Who, What, When, Where, Why, and How. Pick the most important ones. Be concise. Study Strunk and White's classic book *Elements of Style* for guidance in pithy, powerful writing. The use of rhetorical devices is found in memorable speeches. Study rhetorical devices and use them to your advantage. And you will want to add personal stories as well. Use of rhetorical devices and storytelling are both so important in the development and delivery of a memorable speech. I emphasize stories as a separate element of memorable speeches and I have chapters devoted to each.

O is for organization. It is best not to exceed three issues for emphasis in a speech. It is hard for the audience to remember more.

D is for delivery. Pace your delivery. Keep eye contact. Avoid speaking in a monotone voice. Use a dramatic pause at the start of your speech and at key points in the speech. Stand up straight. Scan the audience with your eyes focused on different individuals for separate phrases of the sentence. Don't stare at your text or roll your eyes left and right without focusing on individuals. Smile! Don't look angry or unapproachable. Don't mumble. Avoid "you know," "ahh," and other nervous phrases between sentences. Of course, practice, practice, practice your delivery!

Record yourself on video while practicing your speech. Watch yourself. You will learn what to change in your presentation, both in style and in substance, just by doing that. Those nervous utterances like "umm," and "so," and even nervous tics like rapid eye blinking, lip smacking, or foot tapping will be apparent and your awareness of such nervous tendencies will aid in their elimination. Then have others critique you.

When I teach medical students or train executives on how to give a memorable speech, I have them prepare a two-minute speech on a subject of their choosing. I record them on video delivering the speech and play it back immediately. The exercise of seeing themselves presenting their two-minute speech enhances their self-awareness and leads to marked improvements in their delivery.

It is very important to have a copy of your speech in your possession if you are depending on memory or automated visual stimulation to guide you in your presentation. This is critical in the event of a failure of memory or the breakage of any projection or teleprompting equipment.

A is for action. This is what you want the audience to do. Show what's in it for them, why it is in their best interest to take the action you recommend. Never forget to convince the audience of the impact on them if action is not taken.

Example: "Our country is in need of medical liability reform. Why? Because a broken medical liability system results in less access to medical care. It is in your best interest to become involved. Contact your Representative, contact your Senator, contact your local medical society to see how you might help. Your action is vital because, without reform, you may not be able to find a doctor in your hour of need!" That message lets the audience know the issue is personal to them!

C is for control. Keep control of framing of the issue. Don't let an opponent in a debate, a heckler from the audience, or demonstrators with hostile signs reframe the issue. Keep the topic being discussed as the focus, not some diversion by adversaries. Anticipate hostile questions and be prepared to answer with knowledge, truth, and grace.

CODAC is my expansion of the **C-O-D** acronym from Thomas Montalbo's excellent book, *The Power of Eloquence*.[3]

Stories

Telling stories in a speech is the glue to memory that enhances recall for years to come. People remember stories. A story that is related to your speech's message is the ideal. I give story its own chapter in this book—Chapter 10—because of its importance.

Lessons Learned

- There are four key elements of a memorable speech:
    - Knowledge of topic
    - Passion
    - Presentation skill
    - Stories
- C-O-D-A-C is an organizational tool for developing a skilled presentation:
    - Content
    - Organization
    - Delivery
    - Action
    - Control
- Anticipate hostile questions and even demonstrators during a speech and be prepared to answer with knowledge, truth, and grace.
- Remember, the journey to a standing ovation requires practice, practice, practice!

Chapter 3

ARISTOTLE'S RHETORIC

Nothing is so unbelievable that oratory cannot make it acceptable.

—Cicero

Before you prepare and deliver a speech, you first must decide the purpose of the speech and research the composition of the audience.

Are you planning to entertain only or do you want to persuade the audience to take up a cause and act? Do you want to make them laugh? Or do you want to point out the importance of voting in the next election because you believe the future of America is at risk?

What is the average age of the audience and related preferred modes of communication? With which pop culture era does the majority of the audience most identify? What are the values, opinions, attitudes, and interests of the audience? Do those anticipated to attend have some familiarity with the subject matter or are they inexperienced in the topic? For example, if you are a scientist and speaking to other scientists, then you can use technical terms to describe your new discovery in physics or another scientific field. Otherwise you will want to avoid jargon and instead use plain English.

Rhetoric is communication that is intended to persuade. One important source for understanding rhetoric is Aristotle's writings. As Camille A. Langston explained in her and Lisa LaBracio's "Rhetoric 101" TED-Ed Lesson, "Rhetoric, according to Aristotle, is the art of seeing the available means of persuasion."[1]

The Greek Aristotle, teacher of Alexander the Great, wrote over 2,300 years ago about what he called the three proofs, that is, ethos, pathos, and logos, as three available means of persuading an audience.

Ethos: Highlighting the ethics and credibility of the speaker as a way to persuade the audience to believe what the speaker is saying just because the speaker is who he or she is. For example, a religious leader highly respected for saintly acts utilizes ethos.

Pathos: Appealing to the emotion of the subject matter or the mindset of the audience as a means of persuading the audience to commit to the cause. For example, organizations soliciting contributions for the treatment of children suffering from life-threatening diseases or life-altering conditions, or politicians advocating issues held dear by their potential voters utilize pathos.

Logos: Appealing to the logic of the argument or position as a means of moving the audience to action. For example, a prosecutor demonstrating the fingerprints of the accused on the murder weapon to move the jury to conviction utilizes logos.

A skilled advocate may use all three avenues of persuasion to achieve the desired result!

Any of those or all of those (ethos, pathos, and logos) can be used in the following situations:

1. **Forensic** or judicial situations: where rhetorical skills using information from the past is used to justify a conclusion.
2. **Epideictic** situations: where a demonstration of rhetorical skills is used in a present state of affairs to praise, as in a wedding toast, or to blame, as in some Congressional hearings where it is more theatre than fact finding.
3. **Symbouleutikon** situations: where rhetorical skills are used deliberatively to give alternative futures depending on which of the alternative choices is pursued.[2]

Review other sources for additional perspective on the "Aristotle Model of Communication."[3]

A cautionary note about false information and manipulation of the audience is found at the TED Talks blog discussing Aristotle's theory of the ethos, pathos, and logos contrasting means of persuasive communication:

> But what makes for good deliberative rhetoric, besides the future tense? According to Aristotle, there are three persuasive appeals: ethos, logos and pathos. Ethos is how you convince an audience of your credibility. Logos is the use of logic and reason. This method can employ rhetorical devices such as analogies, examples, and citations of research or statistics. But it's not just facts and figures. It's also the structure and content of the speech itself. The point is to use factual knowledge to convince the audience—but, unfortunately, speakers can also manipulate people with false information that the audience thinks is true. And finally, pathos appeals to emotion, and in our age of mass media, it's often the most effective mode. Pathos is neither inherently good nor bad, but it may be irrational and unpredictable. It can just as easily rally people for peace as incite them to war. Most advertising, from beauty products that promise to relieve our physical insecurities to cars that make us feel powerful, relies on pathos.[4]

Lessons Learned

- Before preparing and delivering a speech, you first must decide the purpose of the speech and research the composition of the audience.
- Rhetoric is communication that is intended to persuade.
- Aristotle's means of persuasion are:

- Ethos: use of ethics and credibility of the speaker
- Pathos: appeal to emotion, for example, a powerful story
- Logos: use of logic and reason to convince
- Any of those or all of those (ethos, pathos, and logos) can be used in the following situations:
  - Forensic: using information from the past to justify a conclusion
  - Epideictic: using information in a present state of affairs to praise (wedding toast) or blame (as in some Congressional hearings)
  - Symbouleutikon: using information to show alternative futures depending on which of the alternative choices is taken
- Beware of the speaker who argues with logic based on false facts.

Chapter 4

LEARN FROM LEADING ADVOCATES, NOW AND IN THE PAST

Words have a magical power. They can bring wither the greatest happiness or deepest despair; they can transfer knowledge from teacher to student; words enable the orator to sway his audience and dictate its decisions. Words are capable of arousing the strongest emotions and prompting all men's actions.

—Sigmund Freud

You can learn important techniques of persuasive speech by studying people who have been successful as advocates. Here are four examples.

A Prosecutor of Nazis:
Robert Houghwout Jackson (1892–1954)

Justice Jackson was an associate justice of the United States Supreme Court and the Chief United States Prosecutor of the Nuremberg trial of Nazis (1945–1946).

"British judge and politician, Norman Birkett, described the first Nuremberg Trial as 'the greatest trial in history.'" That quote is used in a *Stetson Law Review* article that analyzes the rhetoric used by Justice Jackson and provides valuable additional references to the trial.[1]

Here is an excerpt from Justice Jackson's statements in the Nuremberg trial of the Nazis and a commentator's tribute to Jackson:

> . . . in his opening statement, Jackson delivered some of the most powerful words ever uttered in any courtroom: "The wrongs which we seek to condemn and punish have been so calculated, so malignant and so devastating that civilization cannot tolerate their being ignored because it cannot survive their being repeated. That four great nations, flushed with victory and stung with injury, stay the hand of vengeance and voluntarily submit their captive enemies to the judgment of the law is one of the most significant tributes that power has ever paid to reason."[2]

In *The Little Red Book of Leadership Lessons*, my reference source for leadership quotes, I explained that reading also introduces stirring oratory to the emerging leader. You can learn from the past not only what happened but also how leaders organized the facts into a persuasive argument to convince others to agree or follow.

Imagine that you are sitting in the courtroom on July 26, 1946, at Nuremberg, Germany, listening to the closing argument of Robert H. Jackson, chief counsel for the United States in the war crimes trial of Nazi officials. Here are excerpts and the ending:

> In the testimony of each defendant, at some point there was reached the familiar blank wall: Nobody knew anything about what was going on. Time after time we have heard the chorus from the dock:
> "I only heard about these things here for the first time."

These men saw no evil, spoke none, and none was uttered in their presence. This claim might sound very plausible if made by one defendant. But when we put all their stories together, the impression which emerges of the Third Reich, which was to last a thousand years, is ludicrous. If we combine only the stories from the front bench, this is the ridiculous composite picture of Hitler's government that emerges. It was composed of:

A number-two man who knew nothing of the excesses of the Gestapo which he created, and never suspected the Jewish extermination program although he was the signer of over a score of decrees which instituted the persecutions of that race;

A number-three man who was merely an innocent middleman transmitting Hitler's orders without even reading them, like a postman or delivery boy . . . A Gauleiter of Franconia whose occupation was to pour forth filthy writings about the Jews, but who had no idea that anybody would read them.

. . . This may seem like a fantastic exaggeration, but this is what you would in actuality be obliged to conclude if you were to acquit these defendants.

They do protest too much. They deny knowing what was common knowledge.

. . . The only question is whether the defendants' own testimony is to be credited as against the documents and other evidence of their guilt. What, then is their testimony worth?

The fact is that the Nazi habit of economizing in the use of truth pulls the foundations out from under their own defenses. Lying has always been a highly approved Nazi technique. Hitler, in *Mein Kampf*, advocated mendacity as a policy.

. . . Besides outright false statements and doubletalk, there are also other circumventions of truth in the nature of fantastic explanations and absurd professions. Streicher has solemnly maintained that his only thought with respect to the Jews was to resettle them on the island of Madagascar. His reason for destroying synagogues, he blandly said, was only because they were architecturally offensive.

Rosenberg was stated by his counsel to have always had in mind a "chivalrous solution" to the Jewish problem. When it was necessary to remove Schuschnigg after the Anschluss, von Ribbentrop would have had us believe that the Austrian chancellor was resting at a "villa." It was left to cross-examination to reveal that the "villa" was Buchenwald concentration camp.

. . . It is against such a background that these defendants now ask this tribunal to say that they are not guilty of planning, executing, or conspiring to commit this long list of crimes and wrongs. They stand before the record of this trial as bloodstained Gloucester stood by the body of his slain king. He begged of the widow, as they beg of you: "Say I slew them not." And the queen replied, "Then say they were not slain. But dead they are. . . ." If you were to say of these men that they are not guilty, it would be as true to say there has been no war, there are no slain, there has been no crime.

—Robert H. Jackson, Chief Counsel for the United
States in the war crimes trial of Nazi officials[3]

"The International Military Tribunal . . . on 30 September and 1 October, 1946 rendered judgment in the first international criminal assizes in history. It found 19 of the 22 defendants guilty on one or more of the counts of the Indictment, and acquitted 3. It sentenced 12 to death by hanging, 3 to imprisonment for life, and the four others to terms of 10 to 20 years imprisonment."[4]

You can learn more about Justice Jackson at the Robert H. Jackson Center[5] and from a free subscription to Professor John

Q. Barrett's email updates, *The Jackson List*.[6] Also, view Justice Jackson's final report of the International Military Tribunal.[7]

Note Justice Jackson's presentation of horrific facts weaved into a persuasive argument that those on trial were evil who murdered without any conscience and lied about their actions. Adding to the power of the argument is the reference to Shakespeare's scene in *Richard III* where Gloucester begs Lady Ann, "Say I slew them not." Jackson says that is what the defendants are saying. Wishing it did not happen does not make it so.

A Leading Advocate against Burdensome Regulations and Excessive Litigation: Philip K. Howard

Philip K. Howard is an author and Senior Counsel at Covington law firm in New York City.

"He is one of America's leading authorities on government simplification, streamlining regulations, and legal reform, and works closely with public officials, corporate executives, academics, and judges across the country. He has advised numerous national and statewide elected officials of both parties and is a member of President Trump's Strategic and Policy Forum, along with some of America's leading CEO's."[8]

He is a bestselling author and his books include, among others, *The Death of Common Sense* and his 2019 book, *Try Common Sense: Replacing the Failed Ideologies of Right and Left*.

I have known known Philip for almost two decades and, together, we have spoken to audiences in Washington, DC, New Orleans, and elsewhere. He is my friend.

Philip is the driving force of the organization Common Good. His acclaimed TED Talk is referenced in another chapter and has over 700,000 views. On October 27, 2015, I interviewed Philip for a podcast about his passion to get rid of burdensome regulations.[9] In another interview with him on August 30, 2019,

I asked him what he considered important for a memorable speech.

He advised the following for a successful speech:

- Be yourself. Don't try to act like someone else. Be authentic.
- If you are soft-spoken, don't try to change your voice for the speech and copy the voice of someone else.
- Tell the audience what the theme of the speech is at the beginning, so they know what to focus on. Be clear about the topic.
- Give the audience stories. Be specific to the audience.
- Keep your nervous energy. Have a sense of urgency, almost like a bundle of nerves. (I interpreted that to mean you should be passionate.) People want to see the energy and that will translate into energy in the audience.
- Don't read the entire speech to the audience. Very hard to give an impressive speech by reading. You can have notes and you can refer to them during the speech.
- Rewrite each speech. Add metaphors. Don't give an abstract speech.
- Don't worry if you get nervous before a big speech. I thought I was going to have a panic attack just before my TED Talk after watching the other presenters that day. Just know that because you know your topic and practiced the speech, you will do fine.
- Have someone videotape you and look for tics or mannerisms you want to avoid. I went to a speech coach some years ago and he videotaped me speaking. The coach pointed out that I was rocking back and forth from side to side. The solution to that problem was to put one foot in front of the other.

To hear Philip talk about stifling regulations, listen to the excellent *Forbes* magazine podcast where he was interviewed by Steve

Forbes. It was posted online August 26, 2019. He gives examples of absurd obstruction of goals because of stifling regulations and how to change to common sense. The interview starts at three minutes, twenty seconds and ends at forty-three minutes, eleven seconds in the podcast.[10]

A Political Wordsmith Pollster: Dr. Ron Faucheux

Dr. Ron Faucheux, a friend since he first campaigned and won election to the Louisiana House of Representatives in 1976 at age twenty-five, is a nationally respected pollster, writer, and political analyst with a unique background in government, politics, and media.

Ron graduated from Georgetown University's School of Foreign Service. He also holds a PhD in Political Science from the University of New Orleans and a law degree from the LSU Law Center. He taught at Georgetown University and George Washington University.

Author of *Running for Office* and editor of the debate book, *Winning Elections and Campaign Battle Lines*, Ron was a presidential appointment to the National Archives' National Historical Publications and Records Commission. He edited and published *Campaigns & Elections* magazine.

Ron currently is a political analyst for WWL-TV and WWL radio, and writes columns for the New Orleans *Times-Picayune*. He's appeared over three hundred times on national network television programs as an expert analyst and has been interviewed by hundreds of newspapers, radio stations, and magazines across the globe. He frequently is quoted as an authoritative, nonpartisan media source on a range of issues. He also publishes the popular daily newsletter about polling, *Lunchtime Politics*, and writes columns for newspapers in Louisiana and around the nation.[11]

Among his many talents, Ron has an amazing ability to create campaign slogans. He did mine after a few minutes of reflection during my successful campaign for election to the AMA Board in 1996: "A Strong Voice. A Clear Choice." In my reelection campaign three years later, he again came up with a slogan after another few minutes: "A Strong Voice. A Proven Choice."

I interviewed Ron on September 9, 2019. This is his advice for delivering a memorable speech:

- Within the first ten seconds of a speech you need to grab the audience's attention and within the first thirty seconds you need to get them to react positively to you. That can be done with humor or with a startling statement. The audience needs to have reason to believe from the very start that this will be a worthwhile experience for them.
- It's important for the speaker to feel the audience reacting positively. That will give you the confidence to give a better speech and the enthusiasm to make it more interesting with more energy.
- One of the best ways to train for giving speeches is to listen to yourself. Tape a dry run and listen to it twice. Listen to how it sounds. Then, listen to the words and the flow. Can it be better? Can it be shorter and more concise? Can it be more engaging? Funnier? More interesting? What's missing? If you're like most speakers, even experienced ones, any speech or public presentation can be improved. Improving a speech is a process that takes hard work and brutal objectivity.

A Defeater of Big Tobacco: Russ M. Herman

Russ M. Herman is a Tulane Law School graduate who served as President of the Association of Trial Lawyers of America (ATLA) in 1989–1990 and has been honored with multiple trial lawyer awards, including admission to the Trial Lawyers' Hall of Fame in 2010. He served on the "litigation committee for the State of

Louisiana v. American Tobacco Company, Ellis v. RJ Reynolds Tobacco Company (representing the State of California) and Scott v. The American Tobacco Company where he was lead counsel on behalf of a class of Louisiana smokers who were awarded a landmark jury verdict of more than $591,000,000.00."[12]

According to publicjustice.net, Herman "was a lead negotiator in the $265 billion settlement with Big Tobacco, resulting for Louisiana, a $4.5 billion award. He was Lead Counsel and a negotiator in the Vioxx case, resulting in a $4.85 billion settlement."[13] In 2019, he received the Champion of Justice Award from Public Justice.[14]

I have known Russ since we both were young. We have been on opposite sides of some issues like tort reform and we have debated each other vigorously. We are friends.

With his extraordinary success in litigation with large judgments or settlements, it is of value to listen to his views on speeches and the art of persuasion. He is, among other things, a poet and a lover of rhetoric.

I interviewed Russ on September 12, 2019, at his home in New Orleans. For a memorable speech, he said:

- Know your audience.
- The speech has to read well in print.
- Deliver with thunder and lightning. The former is Demosthenes; the latter is Cicero.
- Take care to decide if the speech is a serious one, that is, a call to action. Or a speech to entertain. President Roosevelt's speech at our entrance into World War II was a serious speech. Will Rogers and Mark Twain delivered critical speeches with a great deal of humor. The speech comes from the tools you employ.
- One of the greatest speeches ever delivered was Patrick Henry's speech to the Commonwealth of Virginia. If Virginia doesn't join with Massachusetts, there is no

revolution. One forceful catchphrase, "Give me liberty or give me death."

- The more well-read you are and the more experiences you have in life, the more self-critical you become. The more eclectic you are and the more choices you have, the more you are able to gauge what the audience wants. All play into a memorable speech.

- You must be well-read on the subject matter, sincere, believe in the cause, and have a certain amount of passion for whatever the subject is. The audience is as sophisticated as you are. They are looking for something new, but not a point of view that is dictatorial. Professionals have a hard time separating opinion from the reality of what the subject matter is. They generally don't differentiate opinion from non-opinion but, if they do, they are well accepted.

- If a speaker has not studied Aristotle, Cicero, and the panoply of great orators from Greek and Roman literature—these speeches are recorded in writing—they miss something. Because once you have read great rhetoric and psychology, you get a better feel of how to present, how to agonize it.

- The old English method taught in high school, that is, Introduction, Body, and Conclusion, is a way to organize but it is not the best way to capture an audience.

- A speaker has seventeen to sixty seconds, usually only seventeen to twenty seconds, to capture the audience. It is difficult to do that with a long introduction of the speaker's qualifications and praise received.

- You pick up a lot from fellow members of a speakers' panel.

- Thirty years ago, I prepared a list of rhetorical tools of persuasion and analyzed them, there were about thirty-six. Today there are seventy. It is an ongoing study. My top ones are: Theme Reversal, Rule of Three, Cicero's Dozen Axioms, and Rhyming.

- I also studied Aristotle's rhetoric many times. Five of Cicero's trials are recorded contemporaneously in writing and of about sixty works of Cicero, eight or so are related to persuasion in one way or another.
- Then you have the great battles! Socrates, a phenomenal speaker, a rhetorician. He actually made the speeches against Plato. Plato liked the Philosopher King.
- Study Marcus Aurelius's Meditations and Heraclitus.
- Nothing is permanent except change (see Heraclitus). Your question (of the elements of a memorable speech) is complex. It seems so simple.

In response to the second part of my question, that is, what is the difference in strategy for delivering a memorable speech when you are speaking to a jury and trying to persuade them to your point of view, Russ explained:

- Cicero's Maxims of Persuasion:
    - Understand what reaches the mind and moves the heart
    - Understand motives to understand human behavior
    - Move from the particulars of a case to its universal truths
    - Draw the audience into the story
    - Expose the illogic of the opponent
    - Communicate your passion and logic in the language of the listener
    - Transport
    - Deliver
- Rules of Persuasion from Aristotle to Cicero:
    - Know the audience
    - Understand human behavior

- Place yourself in the mind of the listener
- Bring the audience into a state of identification with the speaker: "Ethos"— Trust, sincerity is the watchword
- Win the confidence of the audience with reason and good will
- Tell and act out the story
- Themes must be convincing
- Master "enthymeme"—similar to an embedded command. Begin with notion of universal belief and link to a certain conclusion—"Ice is frozen; therefore, ice is cold"
- Use aphorisms, fables, stories which lead juror to reach a conclusion
- Clarity is important
- Appeal to emotion
- Honesty, Competency, Power
- Eloquence in presentation is a life-long study. Remember the Trivium:
  - Knowledge: Facts
  - Logic: Reason
  - Rhetoric: Passionate communication to persuade
- Cicero said, "Reading is the wellspring of perfect eloquence . . . (master) philosophy . . . civil law . . . pointed jest . . . amplify the case . . . particular to universal"
- Aristotle gave the Principles of Persuasion:
  - Well-dispose jury to you and ill-dispose to adversary
  - Maximize strengths, disclose but minimize weaknesses
  - Repetition (but need not be same mechanism or words)
  - Emote

- Quintillian, "Institutio Oratoria": He was the first paid professor of rhetoric
- Delivery:
  - Care of the throat
  - Breath control
  - Voice production (i.e., projection)
  - Tone variation
  - Carriage
  - Expression
  - Eyebrow movement
  - Bearing of the neck, chin, and shoulders
  - Gestures
  - Clothing
  - Stance
  - Emotions (tears, laughter)
  - Action of lips
- With voir dire, you get a feel of what motivates them (the prospective jurors). In the tobacco cases, the trial lasted three years. One thousand prospective jurors were examined, and we ended up with sixteen: twelve principal jury members and four alternates. The old Socratic "know thyself" may not be helpful. You have to know them!

Russ then references Shakespeare to show the technique of handling misinformation put forth by an opponent in a debate or a trial:

- In the play *Julius Caesar*, Act III, Scene II, Brutus speaks rhetorically and sounds good (he claims Caesar was ambitious), but it is false as there are no facts. Mark Antony has to first diffuse antagonism to himself. As to Caesar's claimed ambition by Brutus, Mark Antony counters with what Caesar actually did:
  1. He hath brought many captives home to Rome,

2. Whose ransoms did the general coffers fill:
3. Did this in Caesar seem ambitious?
4. When that the poor have cried, Caesar
> hath wept:
> Ambition should be made of sterner stuff . . .
> I thrice presented him a kingly crown,
> Which he did thrice refuse: was this ambition?

- In the tobacco trial, it was fundamental to reverse sixty years of tobacco themes: personal responsibility and everyone knows that stuff is not good. We took away that theme. The president of Philip Morris makes thirty million dollars a year while 400,000 smokers were dying. Doesn't he have personal responsibility for that? He had more knowledge than anyone else.

- Another wonderful tool is "Embedded Command." Defense in O. J. Simpson murder trial used the embedded command of, "If the glove doesn't fit, you must acquit." That is a false embedded command. Prosecution should have followed up with blood and hair samples departing the scene, etc. To use embedded command, you have to be factually correct and it has to be acceptable to individual jurors.

- The most important lesson—rhetoric is passionate communication to persuade!

Lessons Learned

- Reading introduces stirring oratory to the emerging leader. You can learn from the past not only what happened, but also how leaders organized the facts into a persuasive argument to convince others to agree or follow.
- Be yourself, be authentic.
- Know your audience.

- Practice and record your speech. Listen and decide if it can be improved.
- Never forget facts, reason, and passionate communication.
- Give the audience stories. Be specific to the audience.
- Be clear and logical leading to a conclusion that is based on the facts presented.
- Study the advice of Quintillian, including tone variation, gestures, etc.
- Maximize your strengths of argument. Disclose weaknesses, but minimize them.
- Read Shakespeare's *Julius Caesar* and study Mark Antony's funeral oration. Read it again. Learn from it.
- Don't start a speech with thanks to all who introduced you or by listing your accomplishments or praise about you. You have less than a minute to capture the audience. That first minute is the golden minute to get the audience's full attention, don't waste it.

Chapter 5

A SPEECHWRITER'S PLAYBOOK

Oratory is the masterful art. Poetry, painting, music, sculpture, architecture please, thrill, inspire—but oratory rules. The orator dominates those who hear him, convinces their reason, controls their judgment, compels their action. For the time being, he is master.
—David Josiah Brewer, Associate Justice, Supreme Court of the United States (1889–1910)

The best lecture I ever heard on writing a speech occurred on March 9, 2002, at an American Medical Association (AMA) educational session in Los Angeles. The speaker was Rob Friedman.[1] At the time, he was the senior speechwriter for Eli Lily and Company. Prior to that, he was a speechwriter at the American Medical Association (AMA).

The title of Friedman's talk was "Effective Speechwriting." Here are some of the lessons I learned that day.

The goal of a speech is to inform, persuade, motivate, and inspire the audience. Friedman reminded everyone of Cicero's advice about the audience: you want the audience to be attentive, receptive to the message, and well disposed to you as the speaker. Find a way to elevate the audience in furtherance of this goal, for example, praise the audience for some accomplishment.

Friedman discussed strategy of speech and gave five goals of effective speech writing and delivery:

1. Know the purpose of your speech: Who, What, Where, When, and How.
2. Create a bond with the audience, perhaps by complimenting the audience.
3. Tell the audience what you are there to discuss. The old advice of tell them what you are going to tell them, tell them, and then tell them what you told them translates into the structure of Introduction, Body, and Conclusion.
4. Tell a story that helps convey the goal of your speech. Rhetoric is a tool to inform, persuade, motivate, and inspire the audience.
5. Use humor to make a point in your speech but if there is any question about using specific humor, don't use it. The best humor is self-deprecatory.

Friedman suggested five possible ways to organize the body of a speech:

1. Time: Past, Present, Future. The Gettysburg address is an example using time, "Four score and seven years ago . . ."
2. Space: A locality issue, for example, "In this spot, General Custer was killed."
3. Topical: A discussion of a current public event or issue, such as, the voice, choice, and coverage in the health care debate.
4. Problem/Solution: Devote half of the speech to the problem and half to the solution.
5. Metaphor/Analogy: Metaphor is a figure of speech or comparison between two things used to make the point of a speech, but which is not true literally. Analogy compares two different things and points out the similarities.

He also discussed his Six R's:

1. Real: Don't use jargon.

2. Repetition
3. Rhythm: Iambic pentameter, variety, balance, and use of threes, for example, "Will not tire, will not falter, will not fail."
4. Rhetorical tools (discussed in detail in Chapter 8 of this book)
5. Rock and . . .
6. Roll: Writing should be dynamic, vivid, and imaginative. Be specific. Use energetic verbs. Create pictures with language.

Friedman said use of stories in speeches is effective because people remember stories. One example is the story told by President George W. Bush in his speech following 9/11: "We will remember where we were that day . . . I will carry the police shield of George Howard . . . Who died saving others . . ."

As I reflect on Rob's words from that 2002 speech, I am reminded of another of President Bush's speeches following the horrific terrorist attack on September 11, 2001: "We will not waver, we will not tire, we will not falter, and we will not fail. Peace and freedom will prevail." Note the use of rhetorical device anaphora, "We will not . . . We will not . . ." a favorite rhetorical tool of fellow politician Winston Churchill.

Rob is now retired from his position as Senior Director of Executive Communications at Eli Lily, but available for consultation.[2] I interviewed him for this book in September 2019. I asked Rob what he would emphasize as the most critical points for someone trying to give a memorable speech:

Know your point and know your purpose. It is about moving an audience from point A to point B. Don't go there to just inform. Go there to move, to persuade, to inspire. When I get done, what do I want this audience to know or to do? Attention spans are lessening. We are bombarded with all kinds of noise and communications all day long. How do you cut through that and get something done?

I concluded Rob wants the speaker to be bold, not timid. He further mentioned, "Eli Lily became great swinging for the fences, not trying to bunt the ball." After he gave an example of a speech from Eli Lily leadership about the importance of research, he also said:

> In your field of surgery, the best stories about surgery are those where the surgeon saved a life. The parents and patient remember the surgeon and the event the rest of their lives. Something I learned from listening to TED Talks and teaching TED Talks is, tell stories! I like giving people the freedom to explore their own hearts, even one where you are vulnerable. Another big thing is to be human. At AMA, I talked about doctors being heroes.

Rob shared a powerful story told to him by Dr. George Hruza of Missouri about his mother. Dr. Hruza later used this story in his presidential address at the American Academy of Dermatology in 2019:

> She was in a concentration camp in Auschwitz at age nineteen. One day the prisoners were told to exit the barracks and line up outside. All did except a surgeon and the patient he was operating on. A guard told the doctor that he had a choice: go outside or be shot. The doctor said he had to care for his patient and finish the operation. The guard shot and killed the doctor.

Dr. Hruza's mother told her son it was at the moment the doctor refused to abandon his patient that she knew she wanted to be a physician—she wanted what that doctor had. She became a physician. A summary of Dr. Hruza's entire speech can be found online.[3]

If you ever get the opportunity to hear Rob Friedman speak, take it!

Lessons Learned

- The goal of a speech is to inform, persuade, motivate, and inspire the audience.
- Five possible ways to organize the body of a speech are time, space, topical, problem/solution, and metaphor/analogy.
- Remember the Six R's: Real, Repetition, Rhythm, Rhetorical Tools, Rock and Roll.
- The speaker should be bold, not timid, as well as human and vulnerable.
- Stories are effective in speeches because people remember stories.

Chapter 6

THE SPEECHWRITER'S TOOLBOX

The difference between the almost right word and the right word is really a large matter. 'Tis the difference between the lightning bug and the lightning.
—Mark Twain, *The Wit and Wisdom of Mark Twain: A Book of Quotations*

The choice of words and the way words are assembled are critical concerns in a memorable speech. Before writing a speech, it is important to do some research on sentence structure and style.

We are taught the rules of grammar in elementary school. We learn the classification of words in a sentence according to their function, such as noun and verb, and we study forms of sentence structure, for example, simple sentence or compound sentence. As we progress in school we are taught principles of composition. But the real magic comes when we learn to communicate clearly, concisely, and convincingly by polishing our style of writing. My goal in this chapter is to cite learning resources for writing style that will empower you to deliver vivid, memorable speeches.

The classic and my number one choice for sentence style is the gold standard *Elements of Style* by William Strunk Jr. and E. B. White.[1] William Strunk Jr. was a teacher of E. B. White at Cornell University. White used Strunk's teaching notes and Strunk's self-printed book to craft this compact gem on style in writing. After reading this book, you will understand, among other things, the importance of brevity and active voice over passive voice in sentence structure. Above all, it teaches style! It is my view that style combined with story identifies the speaker as one the audience will reward with a standing ovation rather than boredom-induced yawns.

One example from Strunk and White's *Elements of Style* compares writing we often see in modern times to Ecclesiastes:

> Strunk uses George Orwell's example: "I returned and saw under the sun, that the race is not to the swift . . ."
>
> Compared to: "Objective consideration of contemporary phenomena compels the conclusion that success or failure . . ."

The first conveys images in simple words using concrete examples: sun, race, and swift. The second obscures with nonspecific generalization: contemporary phenomena. I recommend Strunk and White's advice; use simple words and concrete examples to make your message understood.

White also wrote a column for *The New Yorker*. He is the author of *Charlotte's Web* and *Stuart Little*. You will gain much insight about the craft of writing by reading other works of E. B. White including *Essays of E. B. White*. In a 1949 essay "Here is New York," you will realize his ability to reflect on the present and chillingly predict an act of terror against the towers of New York City. White wrote,

> ". . . a single flight of planes . . . can quickly end this island fantasy, burn the towers . . . [New York] has a certain clear priority . . . In the mind of whatever perverted dreamer New York must hold a steady, irresistible charm."[2]

Perhaps the evil Osama bin Laden drew his idea for the destruction of September 11, 2001, from this essay.

A list of books and other instructional resources I have found valuable over the years for lessons in writing style that can translate into powerful speeches include:

1. *Elements of Style* by Strunk and White (mentioned earlier)
2. *The Lively Art of Writing* by Lucille Vaughan[3]
3. *The Art of Styling Sentences* by Marie Waddell, Robert Esch, and Roberta Walker[4]
4. *On Writing—A Memoir of the Craft* by Stephen King[5]

   This book gives helpful tips on the writing process and style. A key message of King in this book is to have a writer's toolbox. Those tools include vocabulary, grammar, and dialogue. King gives high praise to Strunk and White's *Elements of Style* as an important resource. When someone sells more than 350 million copies of his novels,[6] perhaps there is something we can learn from his storytelling.
5. *How to Write Best Selling Fiction* by Dean R. Koontz[7]

   This nice man writes suspense thrillers that have sold over 500 million copies.[8] Not only does Koontz tell you important points about how to create interest and suspense, but the last chapter features a twenty-seven page list of authors. He recommends ninety-nine authors you should read and explains vividly what you can learn from each of these multiple authors. A priceless analysis.

   I believe you can apply these tips to your personal stories in speeches. Pick and choose which authors are applicable to your story. As he says in the chapter, "READ, READ, READ." Also, pay special attention to Chapter 4, "Creating a Story Line."

   This book is out of print but if you can find a used copy on the Internet, buy it! On Amazon, third party sellers offered used copies from $224 to $362 in August 2019. Be on the lookout for a copy at used book sales and library sales. It is a treasured possession of mine.
6. *The Fiction Writer's Guide to Dialogue* by John Hough Jr.[9]

This is the best book I ever have read on dialogue. I attended a writer's seminar taught by my friend and masterful storyteller, Tess Gerritsen, whose books have sold more than 25 million copies and inspired the TV series *Rizzoli & Isles*. John Hough gave a day-long course at the preconference event on the topic of dialogue. I was so impressed that I recommended him to Tony Lyons, president of Skyhorse Publishing, my publisher, and Tony contacted John Hough. Thus, *The Fiction Writer's Guide to Dialogue* was born.

Hough points out in Chapter 3 of his book, "Tension is the substance of drama. The moment it disappears, your narrative turns slack." You can learn a lot in this book that will help you in telling stories in your speeches.

7. *On Writing Well* by William Zinsser[10]

This text grew out of the nonfiction course he taught at Yale University. He stresses simplicity and getting rid of clutter in sentences such as a "ponderous euphemism." Zinsser gives high praise to E. B. White's writings.

8. Reader's Digest *Success with Words—A Guide to the American Language*[11]

This 692-page reference book is a must-have resource for writing. It is a staff-written book under project editor David Rattway. It gives correct pronunciation and usages of words, punctuation and definition of words including origin and meaning of words, political terms, narrative, and much more. Be sure to read Rattway's description of alliteration using examples from J. R. R. Tolkien's The Lord of the Rings series and Samuel Taylor Coleridge's "Kubla Khan." It truly is a priceless resource. The only failing, in my opinion, is the lack of an index!

9. *Magill's Quotations in Context, Second Series*[12]

Another treasure trove! This 1,329-page collection of quotations with explanation of the circumstances that form their origin and meaning is one of the cherished books in my collection. One example from the book is the context of the quote "Go Tell the Spartans," a poetic epitaph:

> *Oh passerby, tell Lacedaemonians*
> *That we lie here, obeying their orders.*

Magill explains that Simonides of Ceos won the contest to write an inscription honoring Leonidas and his three hundred Spartans who died at the Pass of Thermopylae.

Another example is the origin of the phrase, "Caverns measureless to man." Magill explains it comes from the beautiful poem "Kubla Khan" by Samuel Taylor Coleridge. Coleridge wrote the fifty-four lines of the poem after awakening from an opium-induced sleep. He started writing but was interrupted and could not remember the rest of the dream! So, the poem remained unfinished while many of its lyrical lines live on independently.

10. *The Great Courses*[13]

These are a series of audio and video courses covering a range of topics. My favorite two video courses on word crafting and storytelling can be downloaded to your computer or phone that accepts the company's app.

- *How to Write Best-Selling Fiction* by James Scott Bell, a writing instructor and award-winning novelist. It has twenty-four thirty-minute lectures.
- *Screenwriting 101: Mastering the Art of Story* by Angus Fletcher, PhD, Professor of English and Film at The Ohio State University and a core faculty member of Project Narrative. This course also has twenty-four thirty-minute lectures.

I interviewed Dr. Angus Fletcher on October 13, 2019, and asked him three questions:

- What are important elements in a memorable speech?
- Are there any subject matters to avoid?
- How to avoid stage fright?

In answer to the first question, Dr. Fletcher focused on storytelling. He said:

> There is not one right way to tell a story, but there is a right way for you. Think about your own storytelling style. Think about the stories you tell your family and friends. Use that style with an audience; otherwise you will be nervous.
>
> The story is a journey. There is an infinite number of ways to tell a story, but each story has three important elements: Beginning—Middle—and End.
>
> Beginning is the way you connect with the audience, e.g., lay out a challenge. Middle is developed by focusing on the goal of the ending. End delivers on the goal for which the Middle provided a foundation, e.g., a heartfelt message reflecting the essence of the story.

To the question of whether there is any subject matter to avoid in a speech, Dr. Fletcher said:

> My advice is the same as that handed down over two thousand years. There is nothing you need to avoid in a speech, but different audiences have different tolerances. So, avoid things that might confuse, aggravate, or offend.
>
> But you shouldn't be afraid to share things of a personal nature. Don't be afraid to share things that might take courage to say in public. Those moments of personal revelation are things that make you vulnerable in public;

things you might be scared to say because of how much it reveals about yourself. Those personal details often turn out to be the most powerful and potent moments in a speech. You don't want to be afraid to show who you are as a speaker.

If in doubt about appropriate subject matter, get advice from someone who knows the audience. Stick with what is appropriate for the audience.

Finally, to the question of how to avoid stage fright, Dr. Fletcher responded:

Most of everything you do as a screenwriter is selling people on an idea. It is public speaking to people who are skeptical. Sell the idea before writing the screenplay.

Acknowledge your emotions when you go on stage. I usually am very scared before I go on stage. I say, "Yes, I am scared" and that relaxes me.

If something goes wrong, or if you are anxious about something, the best way to handle it is to laugh at it. Laughing, self-irony, these are cognitive things that have evolved in the human brain to diffuse tension. Smiling at yourself is always the best stress medicine. Don't get upset. Don't get angry. Don't get frustrated. Just laugh at yourself. And you will find that helps you relax. If worried about something ahead of time, just make a joke of it when you are on stage. And that kind of self-deprecating humor is a good way to bond with the audience and release your own tensions.

Have a conversation with your audience. Talk in a normal voice, don't shout. This, too, will help you relax.

Read and absorb the advice in the above books, videos, and interview from Dr. Fletcher and you will have the tools necessary to craft a memorable speech!

Lessons Learned

- Take Mark Twain's wise advice about the important difference between the almost right word and the right word.
- The choice of words and their assembly are critical elements in a memorable speech.
- Rules and principles of grammar are important to communication in any language but to communicate clearly, concisely, and convincingly, you must polish your style of writing.
- The gold standard for sentence style is *Elements of Style* by William Strunk Jr. and E. B. White. Get it. Study it. Keep it handy when you write.
- Build a library of reference books and video courses after consideration of those I recommend in this chapter.
- Heed the wise advice on storytelling from all, including Dean Koontz's analysis of the writing style of other authors and Stephen King's advice on the writing process and style.
- Read the series of books by Tess Gerritsen, Dean Koontz, and Stephen King to evaluate why their method of storytelling has yielded great success.
- Watch *The Great Courses* video of Dr. Angus Fletcher skillfully explaining screenwriting and the art of the story.

Chapter 7

LIBRARIES AS A RESOURCE

If you want to find out about something, the information is in the reference books—the dictionaries, the encyclopedias, the atlases. If you like to be told a story, the library is the place to go . . . A library is a good place to go when you feel unhappy, for there, in a book, you may find encouragement and comfort. A library is a good place to go when you feel bewildered or undecided, for there, in a book, you may have your question answered. Books are good company, in sad times and happy times, for books are people—people who have managed to stay alive by hiding between the covers of a book.
—E. B. White, *Letters of Note*

Don't overlook libraries as a research resource. Free books to read. Help with research. Available computers to use in many libraries nationwide. Option to download items without physically going to the library. Database availability.

For example, at the Jefferson Parish main library in Metairie, Louisiana, you can locate books by going to historical databases. You can order an item (books and DVDs) online from the library's website. You will receive an automated call when your item is ready for pickup from the library, and they will hold the item for up to three days. Books can be kept for three weeks and you can renew up to three more times if no one else is waiting for the book. The library does interlibrary loans. Loan time depends on the lending library.

I am fortunate to have questions answered by my sister, Marylyn Palmisano Haddican, who serves as the director of the Jefferson Parish Library system at the time of this writing. The collection of the Jefferson Parish Library system contains 866,387 volumes. The library circulates 1,862,830 items per year and it serves a population of 433,676 residents.[1]

Samuel Langhorne Clemens loved libraries. He quit school after the fifth grade and educated himself in libraries. His work on the river led to his pen name of Mark Twain, that is, two fathoms (twelve feet of water depth) that was considered safe for passage of the steamboat.

The founder of Microsoft, Bill Gates, and his wife Melinda French Gates formed the Gates Library Foundation and they donate computers and software for research and writing to the libraries in the US and Canada. They also bring Internet to libraries. Their generosity enhances opportunities for all to research and learn at the library.[2]

A treasure trove of photographic images is the Prints and Photographs division of the Library of Congress in Washington, DC. It is located at 101 Independence Ave, SE, Madison Building, LM 337, Washington, DC 20540-4730. If you need a historical photograph to include in your speech, this is an excellent place to start the search. I have a Reader Card for access to their reading room. It has never been crowded during my visits and the staff are extremely helpful. You can search the collection online and also get help with your inquiry online.[3]

Few Americans I meet know of this national treasure. If you want something as peculiar as, "Grading muskrats while fur buyers and Spanish trappers look on during auction sale on porch of community store in Saint Bernard, Louisiana" from January of 1941, there's no problem.[4]

Or perhaps you desire a copy of images taken in 1935–1936 by Dorothea Lange of Dust Bowl travelers such as of the famous photo she did of a migrant worker with her seven children titled, "Destitute pea pickers in California. Mother of seven children. Age thirty-two. Nipomo, California."[5] Dorothea Lange was one of the photographers hired by the Farm Security Administration. The collection was transferred to the Library of Congress in 1944.[6]

You can order copies of these and other historical images for use in your writing and speeches with the proper attribution. There is a reasonable charge for the copying service.

I encourage you to visit your local library and wander among the stacks of books in the section you have an interest. Sometimes you will find an unexpected treasure for the subject you are researching.

I enjoy visiting the journal section, known as "the stacks," of the Rudolph Matas Medical Library at my alma mater, Tulane University School of Medicine. Paging through the physical journals written in the early 1900s gives me a different perspective on the history and physical case reports. The vivid descriptions in the case reports often provide a sense of being physically present in the amphitheater listening to a favorite professor as they mesmerize the students and residents. The style of many journals today is less poetic—a sterile conformity.

Here is an example of a case report of a patient with pernicious anemia in the *Journal of the American Medical Association* on August 31, 1901.[7]

Mrs. V. J.; aged 39; married; mother of four children; came to the Presbyterian Hospital, Chicago, on July 26. 1900. Her father is living and has had stomach trouble a good deal of his life. Her mother died of paralysis. A maternal aunt died of cancer. There is one brother and seven sisters, all living and in good health. The patient has been obliged to work hard all her life and has not been in good health since the birth of her last child. Two of her children are living and two are dead. One was stillborn.

The author continues with the description of her symptoms:

> Her strength and endurance have been gradually lost. She was overworked during most of the illness, but her legs became finally so weak that she was obliged to remain in bed on and after December, 1899. She and her friends noticed that she was paler than usual, and that the skin had a yellowish tinge. This has increased since she has been in bed. She has noticed that her legs have become much weaker since she went to bed, and that she has not complete control of the bladder.

Mrs. V. J. died and an autopsy was completed. The diagnosis was pernicious anemia. It was not until the 1920s that a treatment was found for pernicious anemia: eating raw liver. Later the substance in liver was named Vitamin B12. George Minot, William Murphy, and George Whipple shared the Nobel Prize in 1934 for their discovery of this cure.

Compare this medical case report from 1901 with current journal descriptions which, although accurate, fail to give you a sense of the patient or doctor as a personality. Some of the patient's life story is lost. And when you review computerized medical records entered through checked boxes on a form, you realize the soul of the patient's history has been stolen.

By contrast, the introduction of the patient in the 1901 journal report creates a sense of Mrs. V. J. as a real person with the vivid description of her family, how hard she worked prior to her illness, and the symptoms she experienced. The colorful description of the patient enhances retention in the memory banks of the minds of those treating Mrs. V. J. and may give clues to the etiology of her underlying deficiency. But, for your purposes as a storyteller, such library adventures into the past style of medical journal publications and medical record documentation can affect your style of writing and your upcoming speech. Audiences respond to stories told in a conversational manner. So, if medicine is not your interest, explore the library collections of your choice and read to inspire the style and substance of the stories you incorporate in your next speech!

Modern libraries also offer access through the magic carpet of the Internet. And what a treasure that is. You can visit libraries and museums all over the world when you are researching your next speech.

I will never forget the first night I accessed the Internet. It was a Friday night in the early to mid-1990s. Back then, my wife, Robin, and I would go to dinner and a movie on Friday evenings after work. I suggested we go out a bit later because I just had received a disc that would give me access to the newly available Internet. Robin patiently rested on the sofa while I connected up though a landline phone and slow modem. Suddenly, I was on the Internet! I was swept into a magical adventure to libraries and museums all over the world. I had lost all sense of time when I realized the sun was coming into the den. I had entered a zone during the night of my first Internet travel while my wife slept on the sofa!

As a researcher, you are empowered with inventions that past generations could not imagine. Make use of this power. Gather fascinating facts and thrill your audience!

Lessons Learned

- Don't overlook public libraries as a research resource for speech writing.
- Learn about access to libraries through the Internet.
- In addition to local libraries, don't forget the National Library of Congress.
- Be sure to visit the Prints and Photographs division of the Library of Congress in Washington, DC. A treasure trove! Check it out online too.
- Make use of the magic carpet of the Internet as a research tool as well.

Chapter 8

RHETORICAL DEVICES MAKE SPEECH SOAR

Rhetoric may be defined as the faculty of observing in any given case the available means of persuasion.
—Aristotle, *The Art of Rhetoric*

In addition to **CODAC**, discussed in Chapter 2, I teach and use rhetorical devices for creating great speeches. Use them to your advantage.

A rhetorical device is an arrangement of words that helps the listener or reader to remember the sentence and the message contained. It could be the repetition of words at the beginning of each paragraph, a question that is not expected to be answered, or many more. The goal is to turn the prose into a message that is pleasing to the ear, akin to poetry.

Memorable speeches are both relevant to the times and melodious to the audience. The latter is important in maintaining popularity in future generations. The use of rhetorical devices helps to captivate the listener with the words you speak because rhetorical devices help your words soar like poetic phrases. As Voltaire said, "Poetry is the music of the soul."

Appositives

A noun or noun phrase that gives another name to the noun next to it.

My cellular phone, a starship, transports me to libraries all over the world.

Parallel Structure
Using the same pattern of words of equal importance.

Thomas Paine writes in *The Crisis*, "What we obtain too cheaply, we esteem too lightly."

I encourage you to read all of *The Crisis*, stirring words at the time of the birth of our nation.

> These are the times that try men's souls; the summer soldier and the sunshine patriot will, in this crisis, shrink from the service of his country; but he that stands it now, deserves the love and thanks of man and woman. Tyranny, like hell, is not easily conquered; yet we have this consolation with us, that the harder the conflict, the more glorious the triumph.

Antithesis Form of Parallel Structure
Using a pattern of words to show the opposite or contrast.

John Milton writes in *Paradise Lost*, "The mind is its own place, and in itself can make a heaven of hell, a hell of heaven."

The Bible (King James Version[1]), Ecclesiastes, Chapter 3:

1. To every thing there is a season, and a time to every purpose under the heaven:
2. A time to be born, and a time to die; a time to plant, and a time to pluck up that which is planted . . .

Rule of Threes
A trio.

The good, the bad, and the ugly.

I came, I saw, I conquered.

Alliteration
Same consonant sounds in successive words.

Examples for brands or companies include Best Buy, Bed Bath & Beyond, PayPal, Coca-Cola, and Krispy Kreme. Alliteration also is found in names of individuals such as Peter Parker, Mickey Mouse, and SpongeBob SquarePants.

Another example is the well-known nursery rhyme: "Peter Piper picked a peck of pickled peppers."[2]

And don't forget Edgar Allen Poe's poem "The Raven":

Once upon a midnight dreary, while I pondered, weak and weary,
Over many a quaint and curious volume of forgotten lore,
While I nodded nearly napping, suddenly there came a tapping.

Brevity

And there is the clarity of brevity:

A World War II pilot in 1942 sent this report: "Sighted sub, sank same."

Anaphora

Repeating a word or phrase at the beginning of sentences. Anaphora is one of my favorite devices and, I suspect, a favorite of many. Anaphora is a rhetorical device you will notice often in speeches once you are familiar with its cadence. It gives emphasis like a chorus in a song, as in a portion of the first sentence of *A Tale of Two Cities* (1859) by Charles Dickens:

It was the best of times, it was the worst of times, it was the age of wisdom, it was the age of foolishness, it was the epoch of belief, it was the epoch of incredulity, it was the season of Light, it was the season of Darkness, it was the spring of hope, it was the winter of despair . . .

And we all recognize these words of the Reverend Martin Luther King Jr. spoken on August 28, 1963, in Washington, DC:

I have a dream that one day this nation will rise up and live out the true meaning of its creed: "We hold these truths to be self-evident: that all men are created equal."

I have a dream that my four little children will one day live in a nation where they will not be judged by the color of their skin but by the content of their character.

And who can forget these words spoken forty years after a heroic epic event:

These are the boys of Pointe-du-Hoc.
These are the men who took the cliffs.
These are the champions who helped free a continent.
These are the heroes who helped end a war.

President Ronald Reagan said this at Pointe du Hoc in Normandy at the 40th Anniversary of D-Day speaking to the Rangers who survived the perilous climb of Pointe du Hoc despite German machine gun fire raining down on them from the top of the cliff.

Another powerful use of anaphora is by abolitionist and journalist William Lloyd Garrison with his words in the inaugural issue of *The Liberator* in 1831.

I am aware that many object to the severity of my language; but is there not cause for severity? I will be as harsh as truth, and as uncompromising as justice. On this subject, I do not wish to think, or speak, or write, with moderation. No! No! Tell a man whose house is on fire to give a moderate alarm; tell him to moderately rescue his wife from the hands of the ravisher; tell the mother to gradually extricate her babe from the fire into which it has fallen;—but urge me not to use moderation in a cause like the present. I am in earnest—I will not equivocate—I will not excuse—I will not retreat a single inch—and I will be heard. The apathy of the people is enough to make every statue leap from its pedestal, and to hasten the resurrection of the dead.[3]

Rhetorical Questions
A question used for effect without expecting an answer.

Famous folk singer Bob Dylan in 1963 used the rhetorical question device with great success in his song, "Blowin' in the Wind": "How many roads must a man walk down . . ."

Latin scholars will recognize Cicero, 3 January 106 BC–7 December 43 BC, in his first Oration against Catiline over two thousand years ago:

"How long, oh Catiline, must we tolerate these abuses?
How long is that madness of yours still to mock us?"

Metaphor
A comparison of two unrelated things as though one is the other even though they are not the same.

Remember Elvis Presley singing, "You ain't nothin' but a hound dog . . ."?

A Combination of Rhetorical Devices
These rhetorical devices can be used alone or in combination. In his *Speech to the House of Commons* on May 13, 1940, Churchill used a combination of Rhetorical Question, Rule of Threes, and Anaphora:

You ask, what is our policy? I can say: It is to wage war, by sea, land and air, with all our might and with all the strength that God can give us; to wage war against a monstrous tyranny, never surpassed in the dark, lamentable catalogue of human crime. That is our policy. You ask, what is our aim? I can answer in one word: It is victory, victory at all costs, victory in spite of all terror, victory, however long and hard the road may be; for without victory, there is no survival.

Imagine a speech you delivered still being quoted as those I have today thirty years later; fifty years later; a hundred years later; five hundred years later. Now that is a memorable speech!

Resources for Studying Rhetorical Tools
Listen to and study great speeches. For examples of speeches considered by American Rhetoric as the top one hundred speeches in American history for the twentieth century, go to American Rhetoric on the Web.[4] The text is at that site for the one hundred speeches, plus .MP3 audio and video for many. The top five of the one hundred speeches are featured in Chapter 12.

Another book you will find of value is *Words That Shook the World: 100 Years of Unforgettable Speeches and Events* by Richard Greene with Florie Brizel.[5] The text of twenty speeches plus an analysis of each is in the book, including Winston's Churchill's speech to the House of Commons, June 18, 1940, which featured the line, "This was their finest hour"; General Douglas MacArthur's *Farewell Address to a Joint Session of Congress* in which he said, "Old soldiers never die . . ." on April 20, 1951; excerpts of President Ronald Reagan's speech at the *Brandenburg Gate in West Berlin on June 12, 1987*, during which he exclaimed, "Mr. Gorbachev, open this gate! Mr. Gorbachev, tear down this wall!"; as well as soaring rhetoric from Barry Goldwater, Rev. Martin Luther King Jr., President John F. Kennedy, and others.

Important advice from *Words That Shook the World: 100 Years of Unforgettable Speeches and Events*:

1. The secret of powerful communication: authenticity.
2. "The secret in writing or giving a speech is to generate emotion. It is through emotion that human beings are moved in their gut and in their heart. And only when

human beings are moved in this way do they change how they think and change what they do. That is the true purpose of public speaking," (p. vii).

There are many more rhetorical devices that can be utilized for speech writing. Jeffery Somers has a nice selection of seventeen devices and a brief definition for them. These include Alliteration, Cacophony, Onomatopoeia, Humor, Anaphora, Meiosis, Hyperbole, Apophasis, Anacoluthon, Chiasmus, Anadiplosis, Dialogismus, Eutreismus, Hypophora, Epeditio, Antiphrasis, and Asterismos.[6]

Another list I came across has twenty-three types of rhetorical devices, including Metaphor and Simile.[7] Sometimes people confuse metaphor and simile. A helpful aid is to remember metaphor compares two things stating one is in effect the other: *Your eyes are the rainbow after a storm.* With simile, look for the comparison using "as" or "like." *Your smile is like the rose that blooms.*

Don't get overwhelmed with all of the possible rhetorical devices. Concentrate on some of the favorites that have been used in memorable speeches over the ages: Appositives, Parallel Structure, Rule of Threes, Anaphora, and Rhetorical Questions. For practice, try writing a speech using one or more of these tried and tested devices and you will be on your way to an attentive audience!

Lessons Learned

- A rhetorical device is an arrangement of words that helps the listener or reader to remember the sentence and the message contained. It is a tool of persuasion.
- My favorite rhetorical devices include Anaphora, Rule of Threes, and a Rhetorical Question.
- Metaphor says one thing is another thing, while simile is a comparison using "like" or "as."

- A study of writings from antiquity, as well as the top one hundred speeches of the twentieth century, will demonstrate the use of rhetorical devices and reveal why these works continue to be quoted.

Chapter 9

IN THE BEGINNING

The first thirty seconds of a speech are critical to capture the audience's interest.

—Donald J. Palmisano

It is critical to get the audience's attention at the start of your speech with a strong beginning that answers what they are thinking: Is this going to be a boring speech that will put me to sleep or will this be a powerful speech that will captivate me?

The first thirty seconds of your speech set the tone for the audience. If you fumble around with papers you brought to the podium or try to move a notebook computer off of the podium or some other distracting action, the audience will tune out.

An excellent example of how *not* to start a speech is illustrated humorously in the first episode of season six of HBO's *Silicon Valley*, which originally aired on October 27, 2019.

The character Richard Hendricks is the head of a startup software company and he nervously testifies about privacy on the Internet before a televised Congressional committee hearing. Because of anxiety, he waits too long before starting to testify and must be reminded to start his presentation. He has four by six inch cards with his notes and they get mixed up. He then stands and starts to walk and talk but he doesn't take the microphone and no one can hear him. He picks up the entire portable podium with the attached microphone and starts to walk but he is tethered by the cord of the microphone. Finally, he goes extemporaneous with microphone accessibility and does an outstanding presentation filled with facts about the leading companies and their methods that violated personal privacy. No slides are used.

Starting with a recitation of your qualifications is sedating to the audience. The person who introduces you or the program brochure usually discloses all the audience needs to know about your qualifications to speak on the topic.

Dispense with the thanks to the people who invited you and the person who introduced you. A simple thank you at the beginning of your speech will suffice.

As you look out at the audience to begin your presentation, consider employing the dramatic pause. Wait about twenty seconds before beginning, while your eyes continue to scan the audience. A dramatic pause before starting your speech has the impact of a conductor stepping to the podium and raising the baton to bring the musicians to attention before the performance begins. As you stand silent before the audience, the stirring quiets and the tension builds as the audience stares back at you wondering what is going to happen next. Have you forgotten your first line? Are you having a stroke? Whatever the audience may be thinking is irrelevant. What is important is that you have gotten their attention.

Whether used at the beginning of a speech to quiet and focus the attention of an audience or in the middle of a speech to allow the audience to reflect on what you just said, Mark Twain describes the technique as "The pause—that impressive silence, that eloquent silence, that geometrically progressive silence which often achieves a desired effect where no combination of words, however felicitous, could accomplishment it."[1]

The first words you utter should grab the attention of the audience. I consider a story an ideal way to start a speech. Personal stores are best because you have experienced the event, rather than reading about it in a book. It is more prudent to tell a story you have lived because books and movies sometimes have the facts wrong.

In the movie *The Longest Day*, the German 155mm cannons at Normandy on D-Day were never found and destroyed. However, in reality First Sergeant Leonard "Bud" Lomell of the 2nd Ranger Battalion found and destroyed by himself, with a sharpshooter Ranger Sergeant Jack Kuhn covering him, all of the 155mm cannons that could devastate any ship in the Allied armada.[2] If you were speaking on the topic and said that the cannons were not found, someone in the audience might challenge you and your credibility would be destroyed for anything else you say during the speech.

If you don't tell a story from personal experience, it is essential that you do research from multiple reliable sources. Also, it is helpful to review the types of sources for the story or material presented: primary (such as original written works or interviews), secondary (encyclopedias, textbooks, etc.), and tertiary sources (abstracts, etc.).[3] It is hard for anyone to challenge a life event that happened to you!

Another technique I find effective for starting a speech is to say a word that the audience thinks is provocative for the occasion. Try to think of a way to say a word that the audience thinks means something else. For example, I do a play on the word "sexy" for a speech on medical ethics.

At several medical school commencement addresses, I walked to the podium and dramatically paused for fifteen to twenty seconds while moving my eyes around the audience. The audience then wonders if I have had a brain freeze or have forgotten my speech. Tension builds. Then I say the acronym "SEC-C." The audience thinks I said "sexy" and everyone is now very alert, including the dean and dignitaries sitting behind me on the stage as they shuffle their feet. The graduates stop texting about the parties that night, and the parents of the graduates look anxious. They are nervously thinking, "Is he going to talk about sex at this graduation?"

Then I state, "SEC-C plus two is my Six Commandments of Medicine. Science, Ethics, Compassion, Courage, plus these two questions: Is this in the patient's best interest? Do I have the patient's informed consent?"

I inform the graduates that if they follow those six commandments when treating patients, they can rest at night knowing they did the very best for their patients.[4]

Other ways to get the attention of the audience include asking a question, telling a story, reciting a quotation, utilizing humor, and more.[5]

My cautionary note about jokes at the start of a speech, or elsewhere in the speech, is to avoid the temptation. Few people can tell jokes in a speech and entertain the audience. Frequently some people are offended by the jokes. It is best to avoid jokes unless something happened to you that truly was humorous and allows you to make fun of yourself. That shows the audience that you are a normal, flawed human and not arrogant. I avoid telling jokes unless the joke is about me.

Here is an example of the audience laughing when I explained what leadership is and how grace under pressure is part of leadership, using myself as the butt of the joke. The moment of self-deprecating humor occurred during a panel discussion at a dinner held at the Robert J. Jackson Center in Jamestown, New York, on August 5, 2009, during the Annual Robert H. Jackson Society Meeting. Earlier in the day at the portion of the meeting held in Chautauqua, I had spoken on the topic of informed consent and its origins from the Nuremberg Doctors' Trial. Just before entering the dining room that evening for the panel discussion of all the speakers from earlier in the day, the panelists were given a glass of wine. I started to say something with the wine in my hand and spilled it all over one of the panelists. Watch the video where I explain how the wine-drenched co-panelist exhibited grace under pressure.[6]

For several years I did risk management lectures for the Southern Medical Association with a skilled professional liability defense attorney, Herbert J. Mang Jr. of Baton Rouge, Louisiana. We traveled around the United States and the Cayman Islands to lecture to physicians and I learned how a speaker can be an expert in the subject matter and funny at the same time. Herb always generates laughs from the audience as he teaches. Unfortunately, that skill is not common. A famous example of that skill is Irving Younger discussing *10 Commandments of Cross Examination.*[7]

Few have the joke-telling skill of the famous late comedian Bob Hope. I once saw Bob Hope speak at a political dinner in New Orleans for forty-five minutes, without notes. He pronounced the local politicians' names correctly and told one-liners about them regarding well-known events that had the audience roaring with laughter. Such comedy genius is rare.

Some speakers use humor effectively to make the main point of their speech. An excellent example is the 2006 TED Talk by Sir Ken Robinson titled, "Do schools kill creativity?" It has been viewed over fifty-eight million times. He advances the premise that kids have their innate creativity quashed by current teaching practices. He effectively uses humor by telling stories.

One of Robinson's examples is about a six-year-old girl who was drawing in class. The teacher asked the child what she was drawing and she replied "God." The teacher responded, "But no one knows what God looks like." The child replied, "They will in a moment."[8]

Here are two stories I used at the start of my AMA Presidential Inaugural Address on June 18, 2003, that held the audience's attention and were published by Vital Speeches of the Day on August 15, 2003:

One hot August day many years ago, a troubled man took hostages at gunpoint in a house in New Orleans. The police arrived. As the gunman looked on, the ranking officer on the scene approached the house and laid his service revolver on the ground. He then walked through the door. At that moment, the troubled man who held the hostages pointed his gun in the policeman's face and said, "Now I am going to kill you."

This policeman raised his right hand—not to ward off a weapon, or to strike a blow—but to feel the gunman's forehead. Calmly, the policeman said, "You have a fever. Let me take you to Charity Hospital."

After a dramatic pause, the gunman gave up his gun, and the policeman, true to his promise, took the troubled man to the hospital. The hostages were unharmed and their lives were saved.

That policeman was my dad, Dominic Palmisano. I only wish that he was alive and here to see this day. But I feel his spirit here with me—with us—tonight.

The side of life he experienced was often far different from the New Orleans of popular myth as the City That Care Forgot. Yet for all these pressures—he remained a rock of integrity and a constant source of wisdom. People respected him, and counted on him. I know I did.

In my first year of medical school, I questioned whether it was within me to succeed as a doctor. But my dad had confidence in me. He told me—"Do your homework—have courage—and don't give up."

Simple words. But powerful instructions for a life worth living. Tonight, I commend this advice to you— as we, as an organization, confront the threats to our profession—and the patients we swear an oath to serve. And I, too, take those words to heart tonight as I accept your charge as president of the AMA.

"Do your homework—have courage—and don't give up."

Many years later, people who heard that speech tell me they remember those two stories and my dad's advice of, "Do your homework, have courage, and don't give up!"

The beginnings of memorable speeches in history are worth

your review because they have stood the test of time. Here are a few examples of speeches with enticing openings for your consideration.

Lou Gehrig's Farewell Speech to Fans at Yankee Stadium

Not all memorable speeches start off with a story, but Lou Gehrig's memorable speech is one that does. He begins his speech by acknowledging a life-changing medical diagnosis, amyotrophic lateral sclerosis, frequently referred to as Lou Gehrig's disease. He then quickly transitions into his belief that, despite his personal tragedy, he is a lucky man. The power of his speech comes from his status as a beloved baseball player who shows no self-pity, but instead expresses gratitude to have devoted fans and to have played with great baseball players.

> Fans, for the past two weeks you have been reading about a bad break I got. Yet today I consider myself the luckiest man on the face of the earth. I have been in ballparks for seventeen years and have never received anything but kindness and encouragement from you fans.
> Look at these grand men. Which of you wouldn't consider it the highlight of his career to associate with them for even one day? [9]

Demosthenes's Third Philippic Speech on Pynx Hill in Athens, Greece, in 341 BC

Demosthenes immediately goes to the heart of Philip's actions against the people. He boldly tells the audience why previous orations against the injustices failed to make a difference, pointing out those who seek favor rather than doing right and those who slander and accuse others just to punish them. He has set the stage to tell them, if they will listen, what needs to be done.

> Many speeches are made, men of Athens, at almost every meeting of the Assembly, with reference to the aggressions which Philip has been committing, ever since he concluded the Peace, not only against yourselves but against all other peoples.
> And I am sure that all would agree, however little they may act on their belief, that our aim, both in speech and in action, should be to cause him to cease from his insolence and to pay the penalty for it . . .
> . . . But if you examine the matter aright, you will find that the chief responsibility rests with those whose aim is to win your favor, not to propose what is best. Some of them, men of Athens, so long as they can maintain the conditions which bring them reputation and influence, take no thought for the future and therefore think that you also should take none, while others, by accusing and slandering those who are actively at work, are simply trying to make the city spend its energies in punishing the members of its own body, and so leave Philip free to say and do what he likes.
> Such political methods as these, familiar to you as they are, are the real causes of the evil . . .[10]

Well-Known and Often Quoted Inaugural Addresses of Two Former Presidents of the United States, Franklin Delano Roosevelt and John Fitzgerald Kennedy

President Franklin D. Roosevelt was first elected President of the United States on November 8, 1932. President Roosevelt assumes leadership of the United States during the Great Depression and at the start of his first inaugural address on March 4, 1933, gives optimism to the people by dramatically stating, ". . . that the only thing we have to fear is fear itself—nameless, unreasoning, unjustified terror which paralyzes needed efforts . . ."[11]

President John F. Kennedy was elected President of the United States on November 8, 1960. His race for the presidency was bitterly fought and narrowly won. In his Inaugural Address on January 20, 1961, President Kennedy starts his speech with words to unite after partisan divide by emphasizing the true meaning of the election, "We observe today not a victory of party, but a celebration of freedom . . ."[12]

Apologia, as Reported by Plato and Translated by Benjamin Jowett

Socrates is put on trial and mounts his own *apologia* (in Greek, *apologia* means defense). As he addresses the jury, Socrates opens powerfully by informing the jurors he does not recognize the man his accusers portray because they speak lies.

> How you have felt, O men of Athens, at hearing the speeches of my accusers, I cannot tell; but I know that their persuasive words almost made me forget who I was—such was the effect of them; and yet they have hardly spoken a word of truth. But many as their falsehoods were, there was one of them which quite amazed me;—I mean when they told you to be upon your guard, and not to let yourselves be deceived by the force of my eloquence. They ought to have been ashamed of saying this, because they were sure to be detected as soon as I opened my lips and displayed my deficiency; they certainly did appear to be most shameless in saying this, unless by the force of eloquence they mean the force of truth; for then I do indeed admit that I am eloquent. But in how different a way from theirs!

Well, as I was saying, they have hardly uttered a word, or not more than a word, of truth; but you shall hear from me the whole truth: not, however, delivered after their manner, in a set oration duly ornamented with words and phrases. No indeed![13]

Lessons Learned

- The first thirty seconds of a speech are critical to gain a favorable impression and to attract the audience's interest in what is to follow.
- Don't distract from your presentation by fumbling with papers or loose index cards containing notes of your speech.
- A dramatic pause of fifteen to twenty seconds before you utter your first words can be effective in quieting the audience and focusing attention on what you are about to say.
- Opening with a well-told story is an effective attention grabber.
- Avoid jokes unless you are skilled at witticism, but the safest style of joke is one that is self-deprecating.
- Study the start of famous speeches, including those examples given in this chapter.

Chapter 10

ONCE UPON A TIME . . .

The most powerful words in English are "tell me a story."
—Pat Conroy, author of *The Prince of Tides* and *The Great Santini*

People remember stories in your speech. The rest fades away. I learned that pearl of wisdom from studying great literature and telling personal stories, and now teach it to students of speech. Who can forget the stories of *The Iliad* and *The Odyssey* having once read the books or heard of these tales of Homer? And when I want to tell a story of a hero, I think of the story detailed in another chapter of the life of my heroic policeman father who rescued hostages and gave wise advice about medical school that has served me well throughout life, that is, Homework; Courage; Never Give Up!

Again, people remember stories. They forget statistics, graphs, and most information on slides.

While stories from news or literature can be stirring, personal stories are authentic and generate an emotional connection between the speaker and his or her audience that is powerful. Include a personal story in your speech whenever possible.

Ideally, the story or stories shared in your speech should relate to the message of your speech. However, the following story proves that people will remember stories while forgetting other details, even when the story is not related to the essence of the speech.

Shortly after entering private practice in 1970, following my tour of duty with the United States Air Force, I began lecturing at Tulane Medical School to give a clinical correlation to the anatomy of the body the medical students were studying. Over thirty years later as President of the American Medical Association, I was giving a speech in Texas to the Texas Medical Association physicians on medical liability reform. At the completion of my speech, a physician walked up to the podium and said he was present as a freshman at Tulane Medical School during one of my clinical correlation lectures.

He said he did not remember anything about my lecture except for one thing: the slide of my recently restored and customized 1971 Mulsanne Blue Corvette I had projected on the screen at the end of my lecture. The car was stolen in a fifteen-minute period when I was away from it and fresh on my mind when I delivered the lecture. So, at the end, I flashed my stolen Corvette on the screen and asked the medical students to contact me immediately if they saw my car on the streets of New Orleans or in any state in which they might practice after graduation.

Decades after my lecture at Tulane, the Texas-based physician and former student said he and his wife thought they spotted my Corvette while driving on an interstate a month before my presentation in Texas. They followed the car to the next exit where the Corvette driver parked in a shopping center parking lot. After waiting until the driver entered a store, they inspected the Corvette. The custom Hat in the Ring design I described in the 1970s lecture could have been removed, but it was unlikely the custom driver seat would be changed. They concluded the seat was standard Corvette and, thus, not my stolen Corvette of yesteryear.

Again, people remember stories! Stories that generate emotion have the equivalent of Velcro stickiness to your long-term memory storage. Researchers use the terms emotional memory, flashbulb memory, and mental time travel and tie enhanced memory of stories to neural coupling, dopamine, and more. Emotion enhances memory.[1-3] For that reason, making an emotional connection with your audience through storytelling is a powerful way to both start your speech and end your speech and, in some cases, for many parts in between.

It has been nearly sixty years since I graduated Tulane Medical School, yet I still recall vividly certain classes because of the stories told by our professors. I may not recall the specific topic taught on any given day, but the stories my professors told are saved permanently to the memory banks of my mind.

Dr. Charles Edward Dunlap was the Chairman of the Department of Pathology. He lectured to us one day in our second year of school. He walked into the classroom and began telling us a recent encounter he had outside of Charity Hospital, located next to Tulane Medical School. One evening while leaving Tulane Medical School dressed in a suit, rather than a lab coat or hospital scrubs, a man ran up to him with a knife and told him, "Your money or your life!" Dr. Dunlap reached into his pocket and pulled out his wallet, saying "I don't have much money in my wallet because I work as a doctor at Tulane and Charity Hospital every day and don't carry much money." The man exclaimed, "Oh, my God, I am sorry. I didn't know you were a doctor at Charity." The man then turned and ran off, leaving the wallet behind. Dr. Dunlap told us that doctors are respected, even by those feeling desperate enough to commit armed robbery. As members of this honored profession, Dr. Dunlap continued, it is our responsibility to continue to bring honor to the profession by practicing the tradition of putting our patients first: care for the sick, heal when possible, and always comfort.

The story of Dr. Dunlap is one I've used at medical school graduation commencement addresses because it is personal to my own medical training and resonates with medical students, their parents, and any others in the audience supporting their decision to choose the profession of medicine. It is a story I've used effectively before audiences of seasoned physicians as well when, because of the onerous and ineffective regulations mandated by bureaucrats who have never treated a patient, the physicians are discouraged and need to be reminded of the importance of their work. It is a story I've used in front of a multitude of audiences because it is authentically my experience, it conveys the message of the importance of, and benefits from, honor and dedication in any chosen profession, and it strikes an emotional chord with the audience because we all want to believe there is a code of honor in human behavior, even among thieves. In this case, it was the awareness that doctors who worked at the famed Charity Hospital of New Orleans were caring for the poor, the destitute, and the most vulnerable of society.

Dr. Oscar Creech Jr. was Chairman of the Department of Surgery at Tulane. He was a brilliant teacher and surgeon. Unfortunately, he died from cancer at age fifty-one in 1967 during my senior year of surgery residency at Tulane. He influenced a pivotal decision in my life through a story he told as he entered the Tulane classroom to lecture.

Dr. Creech arrived at our class at the beginning of our second year of medical school ten minutes late. No one in our class had any intention of leaving because the professor was late. Formality was the rule of the times. The women wore dresses and the men wore dress shirts and ties. No jeans or scrub clothes. We sat patiently. No option to view any video of classes later as can be done now.

Dr. Creech, a famous surgeon and the person who developed the modern technique for correction of an abdominal aortic aneurysm, walked in and said, "I am sorry I am late. I was on my way here and I got a call that a young man, a star athlete in four sports and senior in high school, was in shock. I went to the operating room with him and removed his ruptured spleen. He will recover and lead a normal life."

Wow! At that moment, I changed my medical specialty plans from psychiatry to surgery. Crisis, immediate intervention, and cure! I had found my calling.

Dr. Creech's story is a peek into the life of a surgeon and how events move extremely fast in that field. Knowledge, skill, and immediate response can save lives. It is a perfect story for connecting to medical students as the keynote lecturer during the traditional White Coat Ceremony of welcoming students to medical school. It immerses the medical students into the adventures ahead of them in choosing a specialty. If you are a medical student and don't want the stress of being on emergency call for operations at any time of the day or night, then you pick another specialty for which you feel passionate that allows regular working hours.

But, the message and emotional connection of the Dr. Creech story expands beyond the profession of medicine. It is a story of epiphany that audiences can relate to in any professional path or other challenges they may be facing. It is the moment of knowing what you are destined to do, what decision you must make, and what path you must take! Every person in an audience can relate to that experience or need.

Remember: the primary key to powerful storytelling is to tell a story universally experienced or one the audience can envision experiencing at some time in their lives or at least can empathize with the situation as you have presented it. In other words, the story rings true and is one with which the audience can identify. It doesn't mean that the audience literally identifies, as in having attended medical school in connection with the Dr. Dunlap and Dr. Creech stories. Instead, it means the audience can find a parallel in their own lives with the message of the story.

Stories about politicians usually generate interest in the audience but you must be careful not to anger the supporters of those politicians who may be present. However, the audience always appreciates stories about funny events involving you and the interactions with politicians.

It was the mid-1980s and I was President of the Louisiana State Medical Society (LSMS) for the 1984–1985 term. It was the tradition for a small delegation from the medical society to visit our Louisiana officials in Congress once a year. I went to Washington with the executive director of the medical society and two other physician officers.

We entered the Congressman's office and before we could explain the society's plan for patient-directed affordable health care, the Congressman started talking. He pointed to a beautiful small horse statue on a table in the room where I was seated. The Congressman explained the horse was two thousand years old, priceless, and came from a certain foreign country. He emphasized it was not a gift from a foreign country but rather a "loaned artwork." I concluded he was suggesting it was not a violation of the Emoluments Clause of the U.S. Constitution because it was not a gift, just a loaned priceless work of art.

He then began describing in detail his failing heart condition and his medical treatment at Bethesda Naval Hospital when suddenly his staff said our allotted time with the Congressman was over and we must leave. I always carry a camera so I asked if I could snap a photo of the Congressman to prove we were there. Our executive director, the wonderful Dave Tarver, said I should be in the photo with the Congressman. His chief of staff added, "Hurry!" So, as I quickly stood up and reached across the table to hand my 35mm camera to my colleague, Dr. Daniel "Stormy" Johnson, the hanging strap attached to my camera caught the priceless horse by the neck and tossed it upward!

As the horse from antiquity did somersaults in the air the Congressman tried to say something but only a guttural sound could be heard. I was torn between attending to the Congressman whom I feared might be having a heart attack and lunging for the horse now in free fall. As the horse descended Dr. Johnson fell atop the table and the horse landed safely in his arms!

A collective sigh of relief could be heard from my colleagues. I then hesitantly asked, "Does this mean there will be no photo?" to which the Congressman continued his guttural sounds and pointed frantically to the door. His chief of staff said loudly, "Leave now!" A photo of our delegation standing outside the Congressman's office door was as close to proof of our visit we were going to get!

Here's an example of a great singer connecting with the audience by telling local stories at the start of his band's performance:

The Rolling Stones performed in the Mercedes-Benz Superdome in New Orleans on July 15, 2019. The Superdome is the location for the New Orleans Saints football team home games.

The seventy-five-year-old Mick Jagger, back in top form after a heart valve operation, strode out on the stage and said, "I just came from the ten-yard line—let's hope there's not another no-call." The crowd roared!

Mick was referring to the NFC championship game for the 2018–2019 season between the Saints and Los Angeles Rams where the officials failed to call a widely acknowledged pass interference on the ten-yard line that stopped the Saints' Super Bowl hopes. He also swooned the crowd by saying New Orleans has the best food in the US and cited, "crawfish, jambalaya, and beignets."[4]

Mick Jagger's short stories are a perfect example of doing your homework about the local news when you perform or give a speech. And the Rolling Stones are so good they don't need to do the local stories, but they go all the way with music and local connections. Truly professional!

As Christopher Witt said, "Good speakers tell stories. And great speakers tell great stories. The stories we tell help us define ourselves and what matters to us. They provide meaning and a sense of direction. They touch our imaginations and emotions. They're memorable. In short, I can't understand how anyone—especially a leader—could give a speech without telling a story."[5]

Journalist and Blogger Nayomi Chibana distilled a list of seven storytelling techniques applicable to a range of mediums, including speeches, based on her studies and experience in journalism as well as from her observations of inspiring TED presenters.[6] Storytelling with preferably a personal story makes the list of seven techniques, but she also details how to create suspense, bring life to story characters, show and not tell, build to climax, and end with a positive takeaway. It is an article worth reading.

Comments of others about the importance of stories in speeches:

"Stories constitute the single most powerful weapon in a leader's arsenal."
—Dr. Howard Gardner, professor Harvard University

"Personal Stories are the emotional glue that connects your audience to your message."
—Nancy Duarte, author of *Resonate*

"Over the years I have become convinced that we learn best—and change—from hearing stories that strike a chord within us . . . Those in leadership positions who fail to grasp or use the power of stories risk failure for their companies and for themselves."
—John Kotter, Harvard Business School professor, author of *Leading Change*

"The human species thinks in metaphors and learns through stories."
—Mary Catherine Bateson, anthropologist

"We are lonesome animals. We spend all of our life trying to be less lonesome. One of our ancient methods is to tell a story begging the listener to say—and to feel—'Yes, that is the way it is, or at least that is the way I feel it.' You're not as alone as you thought."
—John Steinbeck, author

Stories often are passed down through generations and make for interesting inclusion in speeches. Everyone has vivid memories of certain events in their life and those events may be related to the topic of your speech and appropriate for the audience you are addressing. We all have a treasure trove of personal stories and it is only a matter of picking a few that the audience can relate to and will advance the message of your speech.

Lessons Learned

- People remember stories in your speech. The rest fades away.
- Always try to tell a story in your speech. Great literature and news can be sources for stories, but personal stories are best because you are the witness of the story and can bring authenticity to its telling.
- The beginning and the end of a speech are ideal locations for stories.
- We all have a treasure trove of personal stories, so pick a few you are comfortable sharing that work for the message of your speech.

Chapter 11

MEMORABLE SPEECHES OF YESTERYEAR

One glance at a book and you hear the voice of another person, perhaps someone dead for 1,000 years. To read is to voyage through time.

—Carl Sagan

Making a memorable speech is made easier by studying great writings. What is it about the writings of certain authors that draws readers and invites repeating in a speech? Let's look at selected passages from long ago to discern why they are so memorable.

The writing of William Shakespeare has been the subject of teachers and students for hundreds of years and captivated audiences in plays and movies. Why is this so? Here is the opinion of one author, Amanda Mabillard:

Shakespeare's ability to summarize the range of human emotions in simple yet profoundly eloquent verse is perhaps the greatest reason for his enduring popularity. If you cannot find words to express how you feel about love or music or growing older, Shakespeare can speak for you. No author in the Western world has penned more beloved passages. Shakespeare's work is the reason John Bartlett compiled the first major book of familiar quotations.

Mabillard then pointed out Shakespeare's "great stories," "compelling characters," and "ability to turn a phrase."[1] The website Shakespeare Online by Amanda Mabillard is an excellent source of information about the life of Shakespeare and his writings.

Let's review a few of Shakespeare's words in unforgettable stories.[2]

Shakespeare's play *Henry V* is a classic, and made famous the phrase "Band of Brothers." The English were outnumbered six to one on the battlefields of Agincourt, forty miles south of Calais, but won the battle on October 25, 1415. Henry V's St. Crispin's Day speech[3] changed the minds of those in Henry's army who wanted to abandon the fight. Here is an excerpt:

> *That he which hath no stomach to this fight,*
> *Let him depart; his passport shall be made,*
> *And crowns for convoy put into his purse;*
> *We would not die in that man's company*
> *That fears his fellowship to die with us . . .*
> *. . . And Crispin Crispian shall ne'er go by,*
> *From this day to the ending of the world,*
> *But we in it shall be remembered—*
> *We few, we happy few, we band of brothers;*
> *For he to-day that sheds his blood with me*
> *Shall be my brother; be he ne'er so vile,*
> *This day shall gentle his condition;*
> *And gentlemen in England now-a-bed*
> *Shall think themselves accurs'd they were not here,*
> *And hold their manhoods cheap whiles any speaks*
> *That fought with us upon Saint Crispin's day.*

Imagine going to the podium with the goal of boosting the spirits of a group in tough times or after a loss of reputation or fortune and you remind them of the value of true friendship by reciting the equivalent of the St. Crispin's Day speech to stir them to action and triumph. A memorable speech indeed!

Or recall Shakespeare's Sonnet XXIX when you are depressed because of adverse circumstances, but your mood elevates with the thought of a true friend who always lends a helping hand and comfort:

> When, in disgrace with fortune and men's eyes,
> I all alone beweep my outcast state,
> And trouble deaf heaven with my bootless cries,
> And look upon myself, and curse my fate,
> Wishing me like to one more rich in hope,
> Featured like him, like him with friends possess'd,
> Desiring this man's art and that man's scope,
> With what I most enjoy contented least;
> Yet in these thoughts myself almost despising,
> Haply I think on thee, and then my state,
> Like to the lark at break of day arising
> From sullen earth, sings hymns at heaven's gate;
> For thy sweet love remember'd such wealth brings
> That then I scorn to change my state with kings.

Or include Shakespeare's Sonnet XVIII, or an adaption of it, in a speech meant to express appreciation to a special person or to a group who did a heroic act:

> Shall I compare thee to a summer's day?
> Thou art more lovely and more temperate:
> Rough winds do shake the darling buds of May,
> And summer's lease hath all too short a date:
> Sometime too hot the eye of heaven shines,
> And often is his gold complexion dimm'd:
> And every fair from fair sometimes declines,
> By chance or nature's changing course untrimm'd;
> But thy eternal summer shall not fade,
> Nor lose possession of that fair thou ow'st;
> Nor shall Death brag thou wander'st in his shade,

> *When in eternal lines to time thou grow'st;*
> *So long as men can breathe, or eyes can see,*
> *So long lives this, and this gives life to thee.*

Or recite these lines from the character Portia from Shakespeare's popular play, *The Merchant of Venice*, Act 4, Scene 1, lines 171–182, if you want to stress forgiveness and reconciliation in your speech.

> *The quality of mercy is not strained,*
> *It droppeth as the gentle rain from heaven*
> *Upon the place beneath: it is twice blessed,*
> *It blesseth him that gives, and him that takes,*
> *'Tis mightiest in the mightiest, it becomes*
> *The throned monarch better than his crown.*

Or, perhaps, you will find helpful the advice of Polonius to his son Laertes in Shakespeare's *Hamlet*, Act I, Scene III, lines 78–82, to shape the message of your speech.

> *. . . Neither a borrower nor a lender be,*
> *For loan oft loses itself and friend,*
> *And borrowing dulls the edge of husbandry.*
> *This above all: to thy own self be true,*
> *And it must follow, as the night the day,*
> *Thou canst not then be false to any man.*

A speech in Shakespeare's *Julius Caesar* delivered by Marc Antony in Act 3, Scene 2 following the murder of Caesar is one of the best, if not the best, example of how a speech can change the mood of the crowd.[4]

Fourth Citizen	What does he say of Brutus?
Third Citizen	He says, for Brutus' sake,
	He finds himself beholding to us all.

Fourth Citizen	'Twere best he speak no harm of Brutus here.
First Citizen	This Caesar was a tyrant.
Third Citizen	Nay, that's certain:
	We are blest that Rome is rid of him . . .
Antony	Friend, Romans, countrymen, lend me your ears;
	I come to bury Caesar, not to praise him.
	The evil that men do lives after them;
	The good is oft interred with their bones;
	So let it be with Caesar. The Noble Brutus
	Hath told you Caesar was ambitious:
	If it were so, it was a grievously fault,
	And grievously hath Caesar answer'd it . . .
	. . . He was my friend, faithful and just to me:
	But Brutus says he was ambitious;
	And Brutus is an honourable man.
	He hath brought many captives home to Rome
	Whose ransoms did the general coffers fill:
	Did this in Caesar seem ambitious?
	When the poor have cried, Caesar hath wept:
	Ambition should be made of sterner stuff:
	Yet Brutus says he was ambitious:
	And Brutus is an honourable man.
	You all did see that on the Lupercal
	I thrice presented him a kingly crown,
	Which he did thrice refuse: was this ambition? . . .
First Citizen	Methinks there is much reason in his sayings.
Second Citizen	It thou consider rightly of the matter,
	Caesar has had great wrong.

The speech continues, and by the end of it, the citizens obviously have changed their view.

First Citizen	O piteous spectacle!
Second Citizen	O noble Caesar!
Third Citizen	O woeful day!

Fourth Citizen	O traitors, villains!
First Citizen	O most bloody sight!
Second Citizen	We will be revenged.
All	Revenge! About! Seek! Burn! Fire! Kill! Slay! Let not a traitor live!
Antony	Stay countrymen.
First Citizen	Peace there! Hear the noble Antony.
Second Citizen	We'll hear him, we'll follow him, we'll die with him.

Knowledge of famous writings of the past has been a great resource for me in speech writing and delivery. I draw upon these works for inspiration, for connecting with an audience through use of well-known poems or prose, for a source of pithy and memorable rephrasing of the message of my speech, and for adding a rhythmic pattern or lyrical sound to my words.

Incorporating poetry and prose into your speech will allow your words to soar. And memorizing a few poems and literary passages will serve as a basis of an impressive impromptu speech if you ever are asked to speak extemporaneously or with only minimal preparation time.

Some years ago, I was on the American Medical Association (AMA) board of trustees and in Chicago for the annual meeting of the AMA House of Delegates. I received a call from the AMA Alliance (the Alliance), the national organization for the spouses of physicians. The Alliance was meeting in Chicago as well, but at a different hotel. Its representative asked if I could do a keynote speech for their delegates. I never turn down the Alliance because of all the good its members do. I said, "Sure, give me the month, day, and time of the speech." "In one hour. Our keynote speaker bailed on us," she replied.

I rushed over to the other hotel in a cab and reflected on what to say in the speech. As I entered the Drake Hotel where the meeting was being held, I noted a large exhibit of the Alliance with multiple presentations, representing each state Alliance chapter, on tables and poster boards. Each state presented its message of the meeting theme, "Hands Are Not for Hitting."

Suddenly, I realized what I could say in the speech to thank them for all of the good work they do. The perfect start of the speech for this occasion was a modification of one of my favorite poems, Sonnet forty-three of Elizabeth Barrett Browning's "How Do I Love Thee?" Upon stepping to the podium to speak, I started:

> How do I love thee? Let me count the ways. I love thee for your *"Hands Are Not for Hitting"* campaign. I love thee for the sacrifices you make when your spouse is called out on an emergency and you have to make sure the kids get to dance practice, baseball practice, and more . . .

After catching the audience's attention within the first thirty seconds of my speech with the help of Elizabeth Barrett Browning, I continued for several verses with the rhythmic expression of gratitude for their contributions to medicine and the community at large. I then updated them on what I had experienced meeting with the public and doing TV and radio shows as president-elect of the American Medical Association, pointing out to the world the importance of patient privacy and medical record confidentiality in addition to the critical need for medical liability reform to keep doctors in practice of medicine so there will be a doctor to treat them or deliver their baby in their hour of need.

The speech was a big hit. It was personal to them. It recognized their leadership and sacrifices. And it sounded melodious to their ears.

I can't stress enough the importance of learning from the master wordsmiths of the past. When something continues to be beloved hundreds of years later, we should analyze why and use those techniques in our present-day speeches. So read, read, and read the classics.

Also, when you read a classic that was written in another language, it is important to find the ideal English translation that maintains the poetry and impact of the original writing. You are not looking for a stilted English translation to copy the style. You want sentences that sound like poetry and excite the audience.

One of my favorite stories is the play *Cyrano de Bergerac* by Edmond Rostand. Rostand wrote in French and there are multiple English translations. The translation considered the best is by Brian Hooker, which was made for the actor Walter Hampden.[5] It is considered the finest English verse translation ever made and it is the version I enjoy. Read the discussion online by Bill Bucko.[6]

Reading *Cyrano* in the Hooker translation gives you a framework for phrases you can use in a speech. As outgoing president of the Louisiana State Medical Society in 1985, I quoted several paragraphs of this translation. Publisher Holt, Rinehart and Winston gave me permission to do so. See the extent of the quote online.[7]

My message in the speech was that the *sine qua non* of quality medical care was to do what was in the patient's best interest. The patient's welfare must be paramount. Therefore, beware of any contract that impedes that duty. I gave the example of the heroic Cyrano when he replied to his friend Le Bret that he would not grovel in the dust or seek the patronage of some great man or calculate and scheme in Act 2. That advice from Cyrano in Rostand's play translated by Hooker made a powerful impression on the audience.

The poem "Ozymandias" by Percy Shelley can be useful when discussing politicians or others who claim their way is the only way and granting them power is the solution to all ills:

> *I met a traveler from an antique land,*
> *Who said: Two vast and trunkless legs of stone*
> *Stand in the desert. Near them, on the sand,*
> *Half sunk, a shattered visage lies, whose frown,*

And wrinkled lip, and sneer of cold command,
Tell that its sculptor well those passions read,
Which yet survive, stamped on these lifeless things,
The hand that mocked them, and the heart that fed:
And on the pedestal these words appear:
"My name is Ozymandias, King of Kings:
Look on my works, ye Mighty, and despair!"
Nothing beside remains. Round the decay
Of that colossal wreck, boundless and bare
The lone and level sands stretch far away.

The style of the poem "Invictus" by William Ernest Henley can be of value when you wish to point out that each of us has to be in control of our own destiny, no matter how onerous the challenges:

Out of the night that covers me,
Black as the Pit from pole to pole
I thank whatever gods may be
For my unconquerable soul.
In the fell clutch of circumstance
I have not winced nor cried aloud.
Under the bludgeonings of chance
My head is bloody, but unbowed.
Beyond this place of wrath and tears
Looms but the horror of the shade,
And yet the menace of the years
Finds, and shall find me, unafraid.
It matters not how strait the gait,
How charged with punishments the scroll,
I am the master of my fate:
I am the captain of my soul.

I have used Henley's "Invictus" and excerpts of the poem "If—" by Rudyard Kipling to advantage in speeches, sometimes excerpts of both in the same speech with my modifications.[8] For example, in my "The Sine Qua Non of Quality Medical Care" speech as outgoing President of the Louisiana State Medical Society in 1985, I closed with the following modifications of Kipling's "If—"and Henley's "Invictus":

> In closing, I would remind you of the beautiful poem by Kipling entitled "If—." It contains many "if" passages; e.g.,

> > *If you can bear to hear the truth you've spoken*
> > *twisted by knaves to make a trap for fools . . .*

> Then he speaks of risk and my modification follows:

> > *If you can risk it all standing up for truth*
> > *And the patient's best interest*
> > *Yours is the Earth and everything that's in it,*
> > *And—which is more—you will be a Doctor*
> > *In the true sense of the word, my son*

> And lastly, to modify Henley's "Invictus":

> > *My goal is to be the master of my fate:*
> > *My goal is to be the captain of my soul.*

Then I ended my speech with:

> You have been patient while I exercised my First Amendment rights. Thank you for allowing me to serve you as president. As my physician friends in Hawaii say: Aloha, Mahalo!

The audience responded with a standing ovation.

Opinions of the courts sometimes have memorable statements that resonate years later to future generations. When I attended law school, my all-time favorite wordsmith was Judge

Benjamin N. Cardozo, who was on the Court of Appeals in New York (the Supreme Court of New York) and later the United States Supreme Court.

He used the following construction of words to decide a case that eventually resulted in the "rescue doctrine":

> Danger invites rescue. The cry of distress is the summons
> to relief.

Note how it demonstrates the advice of Strunk and White's *Elements of Style*: active voice and no unnecessary words. The conclusion of the case is that a rescuer who is injured while saving someone put into danger by another can recover damages from the person who caused the danger.[9]

I use these examples to show how poetry, plays, and other writings of many years ago can be used to advantage as original excerpts or as modified by the speaker for the issue being discussed at the meeting.

Some of the other writings I use for speeches are quotes from memorable speeches or pithy observations of wisdom from the past such as: Theodore Roosevelt's "The Man in the Arena" speech:

> It is not the critic who counts . . . The credit belongs to
> the man who is actually in the arena, whose face is marred
> by dust and sweat and blood . . . who knows the great
> enthusiasms, the great devotions; who spends himself in a
> worthy cause; who at the best knows in the end the triumph
> of high achievement, and . . . if he fails, at least fails while
> daring greatly, so that his place shall never be with those
> cold and timid souls who know neither victory nor defeat.

Another quote from Theodore Roosevelt on the same theme comes from his speech before the Hamilton Club, Chicago, Illinois, on April 10, 1899:

Far better it is to dare mighty things, to win glorious triumphs, even though checkered by failure, than to take rank with those poor spirits who neither enjoy much nor suffer much, because they live in the gray twilight that knows not victory nor defeat.

This quote from Plato in *The Republic*, published in 381 BC, is helpful when encouraging people to vote in elections:

The punishment of wise men who refuse to take part in the affairs of government is to live under the government of unwise men.

Of course, Benjamin Franklin is a source of wisdom when you need a quote for the audience to ponder in a crisis. Here he writes in the Pennsylvania Assembly's reply to the governor in 1755:

Those who give up essential liberty to purchase a little temporary safety deserve neither liberty nor safety.

A quote I have used on more than one occasion when a group was advocating a change in law or policy without adequate study and understanding of all of the problems that would result is the wisdom of Alexander Pope in his "An Essay on Criticism":

A little learning is a dangerous thing.
Drink deep, or taste not the Pierian Spring;
There shallow draughts intoxicate the brain,
and drinking largely sobers us again.

The message is to first look at all the facts and assess the results in countries that have such a policy before making a decision. When preparing the counterargument in opposition of a proposal, I quote Alexander Pope's statement and then give the additional facts of the subject at hand that the governing body or opposing advocate has not presented or considered.

In the book, *Moving Mountains*,[10] Henry M. Boettinger reminded readers of Guy de Maupassant's words about what audiences want:

> Comfort me, Amuse me, Touch me, Make me dream, Make me laugh, Make me weep, Make me shudder, Make me think.

Boettinger opines that audiences still want speakers to move them in all of these ways and appreciate those speakers who try, even if they fail.

So read, read, and read. Seed your mind with eloquence of the past. Then walk on stage and give the audience what Guy de Maupassant said they want: Inspire them. Touch their soul. Make them dream.

Lessons Learned

- A memorable speech is made easier by studying great writings.
- The writings of Shakespeare are a good starting point.
- The study of poetry is helpful to writing sentences that are memorable.
- Even court opinions at times can be helpful in constructing memorable phrases. A good example is Benjamin Cardozo's opinions and books.
- Don't fail to review memorable quotes from famous speeches to help make your point to an audience.
- Take the Guy de Maupassant challenge and dazzle your audience with eloquence drawn from the great writings of yesteryear.

Chapter 12

MEMORABLE SPEECHES IN TIMES OF CRISIS

Memorable speeches are true to humanity; ageless.
—James E. Brown, MD, Donald J. Palmisano's Surgical
Partner and Mentor

Let's look at memorable speeches of the past one hundred years where we also have access to the audio and video of the speech, unlike the speeches of centuries ago. Audio and video of the actual speech allows you to learn also about the pauses, emphasis on words, and other aspects of style.

One website I like to visit is American Rhetoric, which lists their opinion of the top one hundred speeches. You should visit and select some to read. Many will have audio and video. The top five speeches selected by American Rhetoric are from Martin Luther King Jr., John Fitzgerald Kennedy, two speeches by Franklin Delano Roosevelt, and Barbara Charline Jordan.[1]

A couple of the five speeches are referenced elsewhere in this book, but the following illustrative sentences from each show the style and power of their words.

Martin Luther King Jr. at the Lincoln Memorial on August 28, 1963

In the chapter on rhetorical devices, I discuss the powerful anaphora of "I have a dream . . ." used in this speech. Here, I wish to emphasize the logic in these compelling excerpts of paragraphs four and five:

> In a sense we've come to our nation's capital to cash a check. When the architects of our republic wrote the magnificent words of the Constitution and the Declaration of Independence, they were signing a promissory note to which every American was to fall heir. This note was a promise that all men, yes, black men as well as white men, would be guaranteed the "unalienable Rights" of "Life, Liberty and the pursuit of Happiness." It is obvious today that America has defaulted on this promissory note, insofar as her citizens of color are concerned. Instead of honoring this sacred obligation, America has given the Negro people a bad check, a check which has come back marked "insufficient funds."
>
> But we refuse to believe that the bank of justice is bankrupt. We refuse to believe that there are insufficient funds in the great vaults of opportunity of this nation. And so, we've come to cash this check, a check that will give us upon demand the riches of freedom and the security of justice.[2]

John F. Kennedy's Presidential Inaugural Address on January 20, 1961

In paragraphs two through five, President Kennedy points out the election is not the win of a political party, but a win for freedom. He ties his oath to the past, but cautions that the world is different in some ways than at the start of the nation. America has the power for good and evil, but emphasizes our rights do not come from the state. In paragraph four, President Kennedy states we are not amateurs as we have the experience of war and America will fight for human rights. Paragraph five sends out an unequivocal message to friends and foes that American will pay any price for freedom and liberty.

Succinct and powerful messages. No general platitudes.

We observe today not a victory of party, but a celebration of freedom—symbolizing an end, as well as a beginning—signifying renewal, as well as change. For I have sworn before you and Almighty God the same solemn oath our forebears prescribed nearly a century and three-quarters ago.

The world is very different now. For man holds in his mortal hands the power to abolish all forms of human poverty and all forms of human life. And yet the same revolutionary beliefs for which our forebears fought are still at issue around the globe—the belief that the rights of man come not from the generosity of the state, but from the hand of God.

We dare not forget today that we are the heirs of that first revolution. Let the word go forth from this time and place, to friend and foe alike, that the torch has been passed to a new generation of Americans—born in this century, tempered by war, disciplined by a hard and bitter peace, proud of our ancient heritage, and unwilling to witness or permit the slow undoing of those human rights to which this nation has always been committed, and to which we are committed today at home and around the world.

Let every nation know, whether it wishes us well or ill, that we shall pay any price, bear any burden, meet any hardship, support any friend, oppose any foe, to assure the survival and the success of liberty.

This much we pledge—and more.[3]

President Franklin Delano Roosevelt's First Inaugural Address March 4, 1933

President Roosevelt was elected during the Great Depression. His 1933 speech reassures Americans that we will overcome, but it is important to dispel fear. When there is a crisis, people respond to a leader who shows competence and courage. No woe and doom here.

This is preeminently the time to speak the truth, the whole truth, frankly and boldly. Nor need we shrink from honestly facing conditions in our country today. This great Nation will endure, as it has endured, will revive and will prosper.

So, first of all, let me assert my firm belief that the only thing we have to fear is fear itself—nameless, unreasoning, unjustified terror which paralyzes needed efforts to convert retreat into advance. In every dark hour of our national life, a leadership of frankness and of vigor has met with that understanding and support of the people themselves which is essential to victory. And I am convinced that you will again give that support to leadership in these critical days.[4]

President Franklin Delano Roosevelt's Address to the Nation on December 8, 1941

Speech number four chosen by American Rhetoric is again by President Franklin Delano Roosevelt at the time of the Japanese attack on Pearl Harbor in Hawaii, which catapulted America into World War II. The occasion was a world-shaking event on Sunday, December 7, 1941, and President Roosevelt's words galvanized the nation into action. He documents the events proceeding the attack and shows that the bad faith and murderous intent of the attackers. President Roosevelt did not cower or sue for peace in his speech but, instead, said America will overcome and defeat the enemy.

Mr. Vice President, Mr. Speaker, Members of the Senate, and of the House of Representatives:

Yesterday, December 7th, 1941—a date which will live in infamy—the United States of America was suddenly and deliberately attacked by naval and air forces of the Empire of Japan.

The United States was at peace with that nation and, at the solicitation of Japan, was still in conversation with its government and its emperor looking toward the maintenance of peace in the Pacific.

Indeed, one hour after Japanese air squadrons had commenced bombing in the American island of Oahu, the Japanese ambassador to the United States and his colleague delivered to our Secretary of State a formal reply to a recent American message. And while this reply stated that it seemed useless to continue the existing diplomatic negotiations, it contained no threat or hint of war or of armed attack.

It will be recorded that the distance of Hawaii from Japan makes it obvious that the attack was deliberately planned many days or even weeks ago. During the intervening time, the Japanese government has deliberately sought to deceive the United States by false statements and expressions of hope for continued peace.

The attack yesterday on the Hawaiian Islands has caused severe damage to American naval and military forces. I regret to tell you that very many American lives have been lost. In addition, American ships have been reported torpedoed on the high seas between San Francisco and Honolulu.

Yesterday, the Japanese government also launched an attack against Malaya.

Last night, Japanese forces attacked Hong Kong.

Last night, Japanese forces attacked Guam.

Last night, Japanese forces attacked the Philippine Islands.

Last night, the Japanese attacked Wake Island.

And this morning, the Japanese attacked Midway Island.

Later in the speech, he says:

No matter how long it may take us to overcome this premeditated invasion, the American people in their righteous might will win through to absolute victory.

And in the last two paragraphs, he says:

With confidence in our armed forces, with the unbounding determination of our people, we will gain the inevitable triumph—so help us God.

I ask that the Congress declare that since the unprovoked and dastardly attack by Japan on Sunday, December 7th, 1941, a state of war has existed between the United States and the Japanese empire.[5]

In 2019, my wife and I visited the presidential library of Franklin Delano Roosevelt in the Hudson Valley of New York.[6] It was the first presidential library and contains amazing exhibits of World War II. I highly recommend it.

If you ever travel to the Hudson Valley, visit West Point.[7] It is an unforgettable experience.

If you have an interest in the history of World War II, come to my hometown of New Orleans and go to the National World War II museum. It is an amazing museum and it continues to expand. The museum proudly states it is the number one attraction in New Orleans, number three Museum in the US, and number eight museum in the world.[8] Go to the preview of the movie *Beyond All Boundaries* on the museum website. The executive producer was movie star Tom Hanks, who also produced the miniseries *Band of Brothers*. Watch the movie trailer at the website.[9] The movie is shown at the museum multiple times each day. When visiting the museum note the many speeches under wartime conditions and learn the power of immediacy and message construction.

Barbara Jordan's Keynote Speech at the 1976 Democratic National Convention on July 12, 1976

Listen to the audio or watch the video. A powerful speaker with clear enunciation of words. Her message is that all must work together rather than work as a divided nation in special interest groups. She uses the rhetorical device anaphora to advantage with the "I have confidence . . ." repetition. She sets the standard for public officials, in effect stating they can't set a standard for others, yet fail it themselves. She ends the speech quoting a Republican President, Abraham Lincoln. Here are some excerpts:

> And now, what are those of us who are elected public officials supposed to do? We call ourselves "public servants" but I'll tell you this: We as public servants must set an example for the rest of the nation. It is hypocritical for the public official to admonish and exhort the people to uphold the common good if we are derelict in upholding

the common good. More is required—More is required of public officials than slogans and handshakes and press releases. More is required. We must hold ourselves strictly accountable. We must provide the people with a vision of the future . . .

We cannot improve on the system of government handed down to us by the founders of the Republic. There is no way to improve upon that. But what we can do is to find new ways to implement that system and realize our destiny.

Now I began this speech by commenting to you on the uniqueness of a Barbara Jordan making a keynote address. Well I am going to close my speech by quoting a Republican President and I ask you that as you listen to these words of Abraham Lincoln, relate them to the concept of a national community in which every last one of us participates:

"As I would not be a slave, so I would not be a master." This expresses my idea of Democracy. Whatever differs from this, to the extent of the difference, is no Democracy.

Thank you.[10]

President Ronald Reagan on the *Challenger* Shuttle Disaster on January 28, 1986

This is a powerful speech by "The Great Communicator." Note the words he uses to comfort the families and the entire nation. He mentions each astronaut by name and makes the analogy to the pioneering explorer Francis Drake. He gives a life lesson to the children of America and ends the speech with an excerpt from the famous poem "High Flight" by the poet and pilot who died in World War II at age nineteen, John Gillespie Magee Jr.

Ladies and Gentlemen, I'd planned to speak to you tonight to report on the state of the Union, but the events of earlier today have led me to change those plans. Today is a day for mourning and remembering. Nancy and I are pained to the core by the tragedy of the shuttle *Challenger*. We know we share this pain with all of the people of our country. This is truly a national loss.

Nineteen years ago, almost to the day, we lost three astronauts in a terrible accident on the ground. But we've never lost an astronaut in flight. We've never had a tragedy like this.

And perhaps we've forgotten the courage it took for the crew of the shuttle. But they, the *Challenger* Seven, were aware of the dangers, but overcame them and did their jobs brilliantly. We mourn seven heroes: Michael Smith, Dick Scobee, Judith Resnik, Ronald McNair, Ellison Onizuka, Gregory Jarvis, and Christa McAuliffe.

We mourn their loss as a nation together.

For the families of the seven, we cannot bear, as you do, the full impact of this tragedy. But we feel the loss, and we're thinking about you so very much. Your loved ones were daring and brave, and they had that special grace, that special spirit that says, "Give me a challenge, and I'll meet it with joy." They had a hunger to explore the universe and discover its truths. They wished to serve, and they did. They served all of us . . .

. . . And I want to say something to the schoolchildren of America who were watching the live coverage of the shuttle's take-off. I know it's hard to understand, but sometimes painful things like this happen. It's all part of the process of exploration and discovery. It's all part of taking a chance and expanding man's horizons. The future doesn't belong to the fainthearted; it belongs to the brave. The *Challenger* crew was pulling us into the future, and we'll continue to follow them . . .

. . . We'll continue our quest in space. There will be more shuttle flights and more shuttle crews and, yes, more volunteers, more civilians, more teachers in space. Nothing ends here; our hopes and our journeys continue.

I want to add that I wish I could talk to every man and woman who works for NASA, or who worked on this mission and tell them: "Your dedication and professionalism have moved and impressed us for decades. And we know of your anguish. We share it."

There's a coincidence today. On this day three hundred and ninety years ago, the great explorer Sir Francis Drake died aboard ship off the coast of Panama. In his lifetime the great frontiers were the oceans, and a historian later said, "He lived by the sea, died on it, and was buried in it." Well, today, we can say of the *Challenger* crew: Their dedication was, like Drake's, complete.

The crew of the space shuttle *Challenger* honored us by the manner in which they lived their lives. We will never forget them, nor the last time we saw them, this morning, as they prepared for their journey and waved goodbye and "slipped the surly bonds of earth" to "touch the face of God."

Thank you.[11]

Lessons Learned

- Memorable speeches in times of crisis share a hopeful message, are delivered with confidence, and use rhetorical devices, such as anaphora, that add a calming, lyrical tone to the words. Panic is averted, the public is comforted, and a rational solution to the crisis is presented.
- The power and indelibility of Martin Luther King Jr.'s speech at the Lincoln Memorial in 1963 was not just his poetic use of the anaphora rhetorical tool, "I have a

dream," but also his use of logic to persuade others to his point of view.

- Remember to hold every politician "strictly accountable," as enunciated by Barbara Jordan.

Chapter 13

MEMORABLE SPEECHES BY WOMEN

I do not wish [women] to have power over men; but over themselves.
  —Mary Wollstonecraft, English writer, philosopher, and mother of Mary Shelley, author of the classic book, *Frankenstein*

In the previous chapter, I discussed the memorable speech of Barbara Jordan. Here are additional memorable speeches by women.

Queen Elizabeth I, riding a horse, speaking to the troops at Tilbury Camp in 1588 in preparation of the invasion of the Spanish Armada

I know I have the body of a weak, feeble woman; but I have the heart and stomach of a king, and of a king of England too, and think foul scorn that Parma or Spain, or any prince of Europe, should dare to invade the borders of my realm; to which rather than any dishonour shall grow by me, I myself will take up arms, I myself will be your general, judge, and rewarder of every one of your virtues in the field.[1]

The handwritten document of Queen Elizabeth I is available online.

Virginia Woolf, "A Room of One's Own" (1928)

Woolf delivers these words from a fictional woman in her essay "A Room of One's Own" written in 1928 after delivering two lectures on "Women and Fiction" at women's colleges, Newnham College and Girton College, both of the University of Cambridge: "Lock up your libraries if you like," she said, "but there is no gate, no lock, no bolt that you can set upon the freedom of my mind."

Note the powerful message and the style of delivering it with use of the rule of three combined with anaphora: "no gate, no lock, no bolt . . ."

This is the style of writing that, when delivered in a speech, is melodious to the ear and akin to poetry. It will engage the audience, cause them to reflect, and perhaps cause them to become more sensitive to the plights of others facing conscious or unconscious bias.

And note the wisdom in Woolf's lectures "Woman and Fiction" when she states, "Fiction here is likely to contain more truth than fact." Think about that statement for a moment. In fiction, a writer can give full expression to her or his views or give shocking details about an event that actually happened but would cause problems if expressed as fact.[2]

"Freedom or Death" Speech by Emmeline Pankhurst of Great Britain

Emmeline Pankhurst gave this speech on November 13, 1913, in Hartford, Connecticut (British spelling maintained):

We found that all the fine phrases about freedom and liberty were entirely for male consumption, and that they did not in any way apply to women. When it was said taxation without representation is tyranny, when it was "Taxation of men without representation is tyranny," everybody quite calmly accepted the fact that women had to pay taxes and even were sent to prison if they failed to pay them—quite right . . .

They little know what women are. Women are very slow to rouse, but once they are aroused, once they are determined, nothing on earth and nothing in heaven will make women give way; it is impossible . . .[3]

Melinda French Gates, *The Moment of Lift*

Melinda French Gates and her husband Bill Gates will go down in history as the greatest philanthropists ever through their work in the Bill and Melinda Gates Foundation. They do thoughtful, well-reasoned philanthropy in a way the world has never seen before. They investigate a problem, develop a logical solution, and then, very importantly, monitor performance. The lives saved and futures changed are incalculable.

Melinda's 2019 book, *The Moment of Lift*[4] is a must-read, full of personal stories of women in faraway places who are prevented from getting an education and deciding on the size of their family. Melinda's book and speeches share the emotional stories of pain and loss but offer salvation through women getting educated and speaking out. The subtitle of her book is *How Empowering Women Changes the World* and her stories make that point.

Examples of quotes in the book:

- "Love is the most powerful and underused force for change in the world," (p. 113).

- The quote from Killian: "To be known without being loved is terrifying," (p. 149).

The book conveys powerful stories, the essence of memorable speeches and unforgettable books. The child described on page 250—the child who committed suicide after her classmates viciously mocked her when they heard her mother was a sex worker—is unforgettable and it is no wonder why Melinda's husband, Bill, cried on hearing this mournful tale. These are the stories that make a speech memorable.

The Internet offers opportunities to hear many of Melinda's speeches and interviews. I recommend watching her TED Talks.[5] Also note how expertly she handles questions from five individuals on *The View*.[6] She discusses modern-day wealth, feminism, and vaccines. Go to the Melinda and Bill Gates Foundation for her speech on malaria.[7]

Malala Yousafzai's United Nations Speech

On October 9, 2012, fifteen-year-old Malala Yousafzai, a Pakistani activist for the right of women to be educated, was shot in the face and in the left side of her forehead by the Taliban in an assassination attempt. She addressed the United Nations on July 12, 2013:

> The Taliban shot me on the left side of my forehead; they shot my face too. They thought the bullets would silence us but they failed.

She further stated,

> Nothing changed in my life except this: weakness, fear, and hopelessness died . . . and courage was born. I am the

same Malala . . . I am here to speak of the education of every child.

The terrorists are misusing the name of Islam . . . for their own personal benefit.

She said she learned forgiveness from her mother and father.

No one can stop us . . . Let us speak up.[8,9]

At seventeen years of age, Yousafzai received the Nobel Prize, the youngest person to receive that honor. Watch her United Nations speech. She has notes, but powerfully delivers the speech from the heart with occasional glances at her prepared words. Again, a story makes this speech memorable, as hers is emotionally gripping. She received a standing ovation.

The common theme in the above writings and speeches of Woolf, Pankhurst, Gates, and Yousafzai is the courage to stand up and speak out against injustice, to logically point out the harm of unequal treatment of women, and to advocate for change, no matter the size or force of the opposition or the danger.

Moving speeches can be found outside of well-known personalities as well. Eloquence and storytelling are available to all. Life's experience and passion shine brightly no matter the source.

Leah McCormack, MD

Here is one example of a woman dedicated to freedom, a dermatologist who does not take liberty for granted. She reflects on freedom after talking to a dear friend who was a medic in World War II: "Freedom is the sweetness of life. Freedom has to be fought for every day."

The DJP Update link in the notes will take you to a two-minute excerpt of Dr. Leah McCormack's remarks on freedom when receiving the Henry I. Fineberg Award for Distinguished Service to the Medical Society of the State of New York (MSSNY) on April 13, 2019.[10]

Lessons Learned

- The featured speeches by these women are inspiring, show courage, and reflect their love of true liberty.
- Liberty is the absence of coercion. It encompasses the right of women to control their own destiny, make their own decisions, receive an education, and not be coerced by men, or government, or treated as individuals who do not have rights equal to men.
- There is much to learn from these women as you develop your personal style of speaking.

Chapter 14

MEMORABLE SPEECHES FROM THE WEB AND MOVIES

Charles Caleb Colton said, "Imitation is the sincerest form of flattery," and famous speeches can serve as a template for developing your own memorable speech.

—Donald J. Palmisano

Here are memorable speeches featured on YouTube, elsewhere on the Internet, or in movies:

1. Denzel Washington, Academy Award winner, Commencement Address at Dillard University in New Orleans, May 7, 2015. This speech has over nineteen million views as of August 2019.[1]
2. Steve Jobs Commencement Address at Stanford on June 12, 2005. Over thirty-two million views as of August 2019. Note that Jobs told three stories from his life.[2]
3. Bill Gates (William Henry Gates III) Harvard Commencement Address on June 7, 2007. Over five million views on YouTube plus significant additional views at other sites as of August 2019.[3,4] Note how one of the richest men in the world has the audience laughing at the start because he is telling funny stories about himself. This is the ideal way to use humor in a speech, unless you are the reincarnation of the comedian Bob Hope.

Bill Gates dropped out of Harvard to form Microsoft. He and his wife Melinda French Gates have donated over thirty billion dollars to eliminate disease, enhance education, develop and distribute vaccines, and more. I believe they will go down in history as the world's greatest philanthropists.[5]

4. Wentworth Earl Miller III: "The Speech That Will Make You Cry." Over two million views on YouTube as of August 2019. In this story of triumph, a mixed-race gay man who is a movie star and screenwriter tells of his pain and depression while living in the closet that led him to attempt suicide as a teenager. Known for his starring role in the television series *Prison Break*, notable quotes from Miller's speech include, "You only cry for help if you believe there is help to cry for," "Every day was a test and there were a thousand ways to fail," and "Let me be to someone else what no one was to me."[6]

5. Movie speeches—a collection. Over half a million views of the collection on YouTube as of August 2019.[7]

    1. Matthew McConaughey in *We Are Marshall*
    2. Morgan Freeman in *Shawshank Redemption*
    3. Mel Gibson in *Braveheart*
    4. Marisa Tomei in *My Cousin Vinny*
    5. Leonardo DiCaprio in *The Wolf of Wall Street*
    6. Jack Nicholson in *A Few Good Men*
    7. Al Pacino in *Any Given Sunday*
    8. Sylvester Stallone in *Rocky Balboa*
    9. Russell Crowe in *Gladiator*
    10. Lena Headey in *300*
    11. Charlie Chaplin in *The Great Dictator*

Charlie Chaplin in 1940 is Schultz in *The Great Dictator*. While masquerading as the dictator Adenoid Hynkel, and looking like Hitler, he says, in part, that he has a change of heart; denounces dictators; and now advocates freedom: "By the promise of these things, brutes have risen to power. But they lie! They do not fulfill that promise. They never will! Dictators free themselves but they enslave the people!"[8,9]

Chaplin's speech is timeless. It delivers an eternal truth about dictators, freedom, and liberty. Yes, we are not machines to be controlled by others. This was the first talking movie for the famous silent screen star.

It is worthwhile to watch all of these memorable speeches as part of the journey to write and deliver your memorable speech. Note in the commencement speeches if the speaker is using notes and referring to them. You can give a memorable speech even when you refer to notes, despite some commenters stating speeches must be given from memory. Note the authenticity of Wentworth Miller's inspiring speech that self-worth should be independent of the opinion of others. Note the dramatic pause of Matthew McConaughey at the start of his speech in *We are Marshall*. In all of these memorable commencement, personal revelation, and movie speeches note the emotion; the passion; and the use of stories!

Lessons Learned

- Study posted speeches that are considered memorable on the Internet or in movies.
- Watch the following commencement speeches:
  - Denzel Washington's Dillard Commencement Speech
  - Steve Jobs's Stanford Commencement Speech
  - Bill Gates's Harvard Commencement Speech
- Watch actor and screenwriter Wentworth Miller's speech of self-revelation and triumph.

- View all of the above-listed movie speeches to learn dramatic presentation by skilled actors, but these four are a good starting point:
  - Matthew McConaughey's speech in *We Are Marshall*
  - Mel Gibson's speech in *Braveheart*
  - Russell Crowe's speech in *Gladiator* after battle in the Colosseum
  - Charlie Chaplin's speech in *The Dictator*
- Note not only the words, but also the pace, the rhythm, and the emphasis when reviewing the variety of speeches listed in this chapter.

Chapter 15

TED TALKS

There's zero correlation between being the best talker and having the best ideas.
—Susan Cain, "The Power of Introverts"

TED Talks and TEDx events are popular speaking sessions that have been viewed by millions of people in person or online.[1] The TED Talks are global whereas the TEDx events are local community experiences. Both generate large viewing audiences.

Individuals who wish to improve their speaking presentations should watch some of these talks to learn about different speaking styles. Obviously, when a single speech generates over fifty-eight million views, you can assume that the speaker most likely knows how to connect and impress audiences. So, it is worthwhile to view TED Talks and see if you can learn something about style and substance of these popular speakers. Modern technology and the magic of the Internet give you a magic carpet to visit the captured images and voices. Take advantage of this opportunity.

Nearly fifty thousand TED Talks have been given since 2009. The twenty-five most popular TED Talks of all time are listed at the TED website.[2]

Here are the top ten of the TED Talks and TEDx events. Additionally, I have included the presentations by Iranian American comedian Maz Jobrani, twelve-year-old app developer Thomas Suarez, bestselling author and legal activist Philip Howard, and author Susan Cain.

Note the diverse topics and length of speeches. The number of views included is as of summer 2019.

1. Do schools kill creativity?[3]
   - Sir Ken Robinson at TED | February 2006
   - 19 minutes 8 seconds
   - 62,642,845 views

2. Your body language may shape who you are
   - Amy Cuddy at TEDGlobal | 2012
   - 20 minutes 48 seconds
   - 53,380,348 views

3. This is what happens when you respond to spam email
   - James Veitch at TEDGlobal Geneva | December 2005
   - 9 minutes 40 seconds
   - 47,983,430

4. How great leaders inspire action
   - Simon Sinek at TEDxPuget Sound | September 2009
   - 17 minutes 50 seconds
   - 44,998,450 views

5. The power of vulnerability
   - Brené Brown at TEDxHouston | June 2010
   - 20 minutes 5 seconds
   - 42,223,400 views

6. How to speak so people want to listen
   - Julian Treasure at TEDGlobal | 2013
   - 9 minutes 46 seconds
   - 35,719,740 views

7. What makes a good life? Lessons from the longest study on happiness
    - Robert Waldinger TEDxBeaconStreet | November 2015
    - 12 minutes 40 seconds
    - 28,249,347
8. 10 things you didn't know about orgasm
    - Mary Roach at TED2009 | February 2009
    - 16 minutes 25 seconds
    - 27,928,649
9. Looks aren't everything. Believe me, I'm a model
    - Cameron Russell at TEDxMidAtlantic | October 2012
    - 9 minutes 23 seconds
    - 27,423,680 views
10. My stroke of insight
    - Jill Bolte Taylor at TED2008 | February–March 2008
    - 18 minute 23 seconds
    - 23,865,415
11. A Saudi, an Indian, and an Iranian walk into a Qatari bar
    - Maz Jobrani at TEDx Summit in Doha, Qatar | April 2012
    - 6 minutes 56 seconds
    - 13,986,080
12. A 12-year-old app developer
    - Thomas Suarez at TEDxManhattanBeach | October 2011
    - 4 minutes 25 seconds
    - 9,608,895 views
13. Four ways to fix a broken legal system
    - Philip Howard at TED2010 | February 2010
    - 18 minutes
    - 704,526 views

14. The power of introverts
- Susan Cain at TED2012 | February–March 2012
- 18 minutes
- 24,700,594 views, and now in the top ten as of December 9, 2019

An important lesson from a study of TED Talks is the imperative to tell a story. Remember, it is my belief that a story is the best way to have the audience remember your talk years later.

One analysis[4] of TED Talks found the following:

TED talks that go viral are made up of
- 65% personal stories
- 25% data, facts, and figures
- 10% resume builders to reinforce speaker credibility

A mandatory rule of TED Talks and TEDx is the talk cannot exceed eighteen minutes. You will note in the top ten wonderful TED Talk of Sir Ken Robinson at TED February 2006 that he spoke for nineteen minutes eight seconds, but eighteen minutes maximum length is the general rule.

Why a limit of eighteen minutes for these popular speeches? Carmine Gallo pointed out that TED curator Chris Anderson explained the organization's thinking this way:[5]

It [18 minutes] is long enough to be serious and short enough to hold people's attention. It turns out that this length also works incredibly well online. It's the length of a coffee break. So, you watch a great talk, and forward the link to two or three people. It can go viral, very easily. The 18-minute length also works much like the way Twitter forces people to be disciplined in what they write. By forcing speakers who are used to going on for 45 minutes to bring it down to 18, you get them to really think about what they want to say. What is the key point they want to communicate? It has a clarifying effect. It brings discipline.

When I am invited to give a keynote speech, the expectation is a speech of forty-five to fifty minutes with another ten to fifteen minutes following the speech for questions and answers. If I am invited to give an after-dinner or luncheon speech at a meeting, the usual allotted time is thirty minutes plus additional time for a few questions and answers. Though the popular TED Talks allow only eighteen minutes, you should be prepared for thirty-minute and sixty-minute speech opportunities.

You can learn speech writing tips from watching TED Talks, even though they are shorter than your speech is likely to be. Keep in mind that the shorter the speech, the harder it is to write the speech and still get your points across. The shorter speech forces you to focus on the important points of your message.

Different rules for different scenarios, but you must be prepared no matter the venue. It is critical that you tailor your speech to the time allotted and practice it enough so that you stay within the time limits.

Didn't Get Invited to Do a TED Talk? Vlog!

Vlogging is a passport to a worldwide audience.
—Donald J. Palmisano

If your teaching and entertainment skills have not been recognized yet by the world and TED Talks did not call you, there is an alternative: vlogging! You can potentially gain fame and fortune by cultivating a large number of followers and selling ads. Or you may get invited to do speeches with significant honorariums. Or it may just be a venue to practice your speaking skills. Nothing ventured, nothing gained.

A few definitions first about posting on the Internet:

- Blog is the posting of a written commentary
- Podcast is the posting of an audio lecture
- Vlog is the posting of a video

To be a successful vlogger, you should learn excellent presentation skills and do a quality technical recording of audio and video. Reread all the chapters in this book. Study techniques on the Internet.[6–8] Good luck!

Lessons Learned

- TED Talks and TEDx events are good resources to study speeches. You can see how popular the talks are by checking the number of times they have been viewed.
- TED Talks and TEDx events are eighteen minutes or less.
- You should be prepared to give speeches of varying lengths if you wish to speak at conventions, meetings, or presentations.
- Edit and practice your speech as much as needed to stay within the allotted time.
- The Internet is your galaxy of opportunity if you decide to vlog.
- Make sure your postings are high quality and add wisdom in some form.
- Remember that any posting to the Internet remains somewhere in cyberspace forever. Don't embarrass yourself or others.

Chapter 16

EXPERIMENTAL WRITINGS AS PART OF A SPEECH

Poetry is a balm for hurts of old, never told; it is the Philosopher's Stone to happiness.

—Donald J. Palmisano

Quoting poetry during a speech can drive home a point and awaken memories long dormant in the audience. I gave the example of modifying the famous poem, "How Do I Love Thee?" by Elizabeth Barrett Browning when I was called on short notice to substitute for a keynote speaker in Chapter 11.

But what of inserting your own poetry into a speech? This is akin to joke-telling. It can be great if you are a famous comic or poet. However, if you are not, it is best to use beloved poems that have endured for hundreds of years.

Here are two examples below of my poetry that I have not used in a speech, even though one, "Murder Stalks the City," was published in the *Orleans Parish Medical Society Bulletin* years ago. Perhaps one day I will place one or both in a speech if the subject matter is appropriate for the theme of the meeting, for instance, illicit drugs, murder, or suicide.

The message here is stick to the proven hits. However, there is another adage: no risk, no gain! Your choice.

"MURDER STALKS THE CITY" (1980)
A bullet spent

A life taken
A lonely widow weeps
A child, too young to understand, only knows he will
    never hear his loving father
Laugh again nor see him throw another football pass
Now the killer with his loot
Buys the poison to soothe his fire
The pusher cares not the origin of his bounty,
He speeds away in his fancy chariot.
Will Justice awake from the slumber?
Will one day the evil and not just the good
    feed the crow before their time?
Time moves,
The good buy locks,
The good buy guns,
They watch.
They wait.

"STRANGER ON THE LEVEE" (1981)
One night on the levee,
A stranger debarked from the ferry
This is what he said to me:
Echoes haunt me,
Specters stalk me.
At sunrise his body washed ashore,
A note said, "I can't stand it anymore."

For a happier message, this is a poem I wrote years ago and
modified recently on my eightieth birthday for friends who helped
me over the years. Such a poem showed my heartfelt appreciation
to those who were true friends in bad times as well as good times.
If you make yourself vulnerable and express appreciation to dear
friends, your efforts will be appreciated. This same reasoning
applies to an audience when you deliver your keynote address.

"ODE TO FRIENDS OF TRUE WORTH" (2019)
In man's journey upon this Earth
a few are blest with friends of true worth.
Ah, but the rub is to know who is friend
   and who is foe
   and who is neither.
It will never be known to the casual reader,
nor will it be known in times of plenty
for then apparent friends are many.
But at times of distress
there may come a blessing in disguise
leading to a priceless prize
of identity of friends; friends of true worth.
And so, in thanks to my friends gathered tonight
in celebration of my 80 years of life
I write to acknowledge your unwavering help.
I am grateful for your friendship,
your enrichment of my life
and your wise counsel no matter the day or hour.
May your days be filled with mirth
and your nights with restful slumber
I salute you my friends, my friends of true worth!

Lessons Learned

- Quoting poetry can make a point and awaken memories long dormant in the mind.
- Be selective with personal poetry, just as you should be with jokes.

Chapter 17

TO PROJECT OR NOT TO PROJECT . . . THAT IS THE QUESTION

There were no audiovisuals used in history's most eloquent speeches.

—Donald J. Palmisano

Based on my many years of public speaking, I reject the theory that most presentations can be enhanced by the use of audiovisual aids. Instead, I teach that audiovisual aids are useful only when a sound or visual image increases the comprehension of the subject matter more than the spoken word alone.

Too often, conference speakers project the same words they are saying on their slides to the audience just because they think the use of audiovisual support is essential to being a good speaker. Text on a series of slides rarely enhances the quality of a speech and too often prevents the speech from feeling dynamic, because the audience is staring at the slides rather than connecting with the speaker.

Sure, I am tempted to succumb to the pressure of that looming speaker evaluation form that rates the use of audiovisual aids and defaults to zero if none were used, lowering the speaker's overall score; but I use audiovisual support during my speeches and lectures only when I am certain it will add to the thrust of my words.

I rarely use projected images in any format and I typically ask that any handout I prepare be distributed at the end of my lecture. A handout describing the more detailed aspects of persuasive speech theory, speech preparation guidance, or speech delivery tips can be a helpful reference for the serious student of public speaking, but a handout should not be a distraction from fully engaging with the speaker. Distributing the handout at the end of the speech ensures the audience is not reading the handout instead of viewing the live presentation.

With modern audiovisual equipment, projection of a visual image may not require dimming of the lights. However, if required, turning out the lights to show slides or a video can set off a reflex in the audience. As one wag said, lights out means time for sleep or sex. Obviously, sex is not going to occur, but as lights dim, people's minds often wander and, if tired, they may drift off to sleep.

Remember, every time those in the audience are looking at a slide, they are not looking at you! So, unless the message is something you cannot verbalize as well as a visual image, keep the audience focused on you and your animated speech. Otherwise, slides or videos are just one more thing that can go wrong and ruin your presentation.

Of course, slides are helpful in some limited circumstances. A speech on great works of art undoubtedly would benefit from displaying the visual images of such art. A lecture on human anatomy would be much easier to grasp if provided with images of internal organs.

I use slides to show medical operation images such as the appearance of the rarity of two gallbladders nestled under the liver before I removed both from a patient during an operation. Also, a slide to show an ulcer in the neck artery that was the source of an embolus to the brain causing a stroke is better than the thousand words that would be necessary to describe the "pothole" in the neck without slides.

Another time I use slides is when I am speaking about the devastation of Hurricane Katrina in my hometown of New Orleans and related survival tips during and after the storm's destruction.

Slides and images may be useful in some business situations as well. A graph showing a trend over the past ten years will have more impact than verbally describing the data. Also, a slide of an architectural rendering of the proposed new headquarters of a company would aid in announcing the change.

Slides are useful as proof of a discovery as well. Once I showed one slide while presenting in New Orleans on the topic of how to give a memorable speech to an audience of international insurance brokers. I used the solo slide to emphasize slides should be avoided unless they are critical to the message of the presentation or to document that an unusual event just occurred such as the spotting of an unidentified flying object (UFO). My single slide was a drawing of the underside of the wings of two birds, one the Pileated Woodpecker and the other the Ivory-billed Woodpecker. The Ivory-Billed Woodpecker, the larger of the two woodpeckers, has a distinctive white undersurface of the wings with "only a narrow, wedge-shaped black strip down the central part of the wing."[1] That is a key feature to distinguish the two birds who have been misidentified by some in the past because of their similar appearance.

I encouraged the audience of international insurance brokers to try to spot the once-thought extinct Ivory-Billed Woodpecker while near the Atchafalaya Basin on the skirts of New Orleans because he or she would be famous if successful. I also took the opportunity to use the slide to weave in a local story about the efforts of a Louisiana state representative to stake claim on the spotting of the rare, if not extinct, Ivory-Billed Woodpecker.

The Ivory-Billed Woodpecker was declared extinct in 1932. That same year, a Louisiana state representative spotted one while hunting, shot it, and then brought the dead bird to the Louisiana Wildlife Department to prove it was not extinct! The last sighting was in 1944 of a female Ivory-Billed in the Singer Tract in Madison Parish, Louisiana. No confirmed sightings have been made since that time.[2]

A well-chosen story to compliment a slide, or even a story

minus the slide, rarely is forgotten by the audience. Well-crafted and delivered stories are invaluable to connect the audience to the purpose of your speech and to engage their brains in a manner that allows retention of the information. By contrast, a speech delivered through a text-driven slideshow provides little emotional attachment and its intended message fades from memory quickly.

I hold the same opinion regarding videos. Use videos only when they more powerful than words alone. An example of one video I use for certain speeches or panel discussions is the ten-minute *Beyond Blame*, a powerful emotional documentary of three professionals who made medication errors that caused the death of their patients. The three individuals are interviewed, with the goal to move from shame and blame to a culture of finding the root cause of the accident and change the system so it doesn't happen again. The video is available for purchase at the Institute for Safe Medication Practices.[3]

If you do use slides or videos, learn how to put together presentations with outstanding visuals and continue to look at the audience most of the time. Don't use too much text or otherwise crowd too much information onto the slide. Make certain the font is large enough and the contrast visually pleasing so that everyone in the room, including someone in the last row, can read the slide. Don't use animation that adds nothing to your message and only serves to distract from what you or the slide is saying. Don't rely on your slides to inform you on what to say. You should know the material separate from your slideshows.

The best slide (PowerPoint) presentations I have ever witnessed were delivered by Dr. Richard Anderson, CEO and Chair of The Doctors Company (TDC) in Napa, California. The slides complemented his speech and Dr. Anderson prepared for his presentations so well that he didn't need to read the slides to his audience. Well-designed graphs demonstrated performance over multiple years. I watched him do those outstanding presentations during the fifteen years I served as a board member of TDC. Such skills are rare, but all can work toward this goal.

Of course, not all audiovisual issues in speech delivery are related to visual projections. I sometimes am asked by the audiovisual personnel if I am going to stand behind a podium or walk around the stage while delivering my speech. That question may be relevant for choice and placement of the microphone or to anticipate camera angles if the presentation is being recorded. One audiovisual department employee even commented to me that all successful speakers walk around the stage while speaking. My response was, "Today you will see one who doesn't!"

If given options, you must decide what position on the stage is most comfortable to you. Success is not predicated on whether you stand behind a podium or walk around a stage while delivering your speech. Standing ovations occur when you know your subject matter, tell compelling stories, and speak with passion. You should decide whether you give your best performance standing behind a podium, standing in the middle of the stage without a podium, sitting on a stool placed on the stage, or walking around the stage. Of course, your decision should take into account where you can discretely place your back up notes should your mind go blank or audiovisual support fail.

Lessons Learned

- A key decision in delivering a speech is whether to use audiovisual aids as part of your presentation, such as written outlines of your speech or visual image projections.
- While not essential to a memorable speech, slides can enhance a presentation in some instances, such as if the speech references great works of art, before and after photographs of plastic surgery, showing trends in business, presenting images of a disaster that words alone cannot describe, and as proof of a rare find.
- An advantage of not using projection slides or videos is that this absence focuses the audience's attention on the

speaker and also eliminates equipment failure concerns. Never forget that some of the most celebrated speeches in history were done from a podium without visual image projections, including those from John F. Kennedy, Martin Luther King Jr., and Ronald Reagan.

Chapter 18

A FEW WORDS ABOUT THE TELEPROMPTER

Anything that can go wrong, will go wrong.
—Murphy's Law

There are occasions when you will be asked to use a teleprompter. One reason for this might be that there is a strict time limit for the entire program and the use of a teleprompter will force the speaker to stay on script. Another reason is to have a security blanket for the speaker if panic sets in.

The American Medical Association (AMA) has a one-hour program for the inauguration of the incoming president. In that one hour, all of the presidents of the state medical associations, some specialty associations and alliances, and the AMA Board and Executive Vice President are introduced. A prayer is offered. The outgoing president gives a short farewell speech and the incoming president takes the oath of office and delivers a thirty-minute address following a musical interlude of about ten to fifteen minutes by a person or group selected by the incoming president. Thus, the presidential address has to be timed and delivered in the last thirty minutes.

A practiced teleprompter speech almost guarantees the time limit will be observed, however, the teleprompter can make a speaker appear robotic if she or he does not learn some simple but effective techniques of use.

Thanks to AMA, I fortunately received training in the use

of the teleprompter by the famous trainer Michael Sheehan of Sheehan and Associates on April 14, 2003, in Washington, DC. Mr. Sheehan has coached American presidents for their inaugural addresses.

The most important point I can give you is to not act like a metronome in a piano practice. Do not go back and forth between the two teleprompter screens in a robotic sequence: right . . . left . . . right . . . left . . . You will not look natural and you may hypnotize the audience or put them to sleep.

The proper way to look back and forth between the two teleprompter screens is to break up the sequence with a lob to the middle of the audience akin to hitting the tennis ball over the middle of the net after the side-to-side returns of the ball. After the lob, you may go back to the preceding screen. In short, mix it up!

And don't forget to look at people in the audience. Pick out a person and look directly at that person while saying a phase such as "Do your homework!" . . . then move to another person, lock eyes, and say, "Have courage!" . . . and finally, go to a third person, perhaps on the other side of the room, and say the third part of the secret to success my dad taught me, "and don't give up!"

There will be parts of your speech you have burned into your memory for which you don't need the teleprompter or the paper copy of your speech to deliver. Those are the best times to look away from the teleprompter and directly at the audience.

As I always stress, carry a copy of your speech with you even when you are using a teleprompter. Why? Good risk management! If the teleprompter fails or the person controlling it puts the wrong speech on the screen, or, heaven forbid, the teleprompter operator gets ill, you are prepared. Does this ever happen?

A well-known example is President Clinton delivering a speech to a joint session of Congress in 1993 when the wrong speech was put on the teleprompter. He then had to go on his own for a while. I don't know what the repercussions were for the unfortunate teleprompter operator. He recalled that failure obliquely when he later gave his first State of the Union address on January 25, 1994, by saying:

> Mr. Speaker, Mr. President, members of the 103rd Congress, my fellow Americans . . . I'm not at all sure what speech is in the teleprompter tonight, but I hope we can talk about the State of the Union.[1, 2]

Another example of a teleprompter failure is President Reagan's speech before the European Parliament on May 8, 1985. The teleprompter "cut out three times, causing the President to lose his place."[3]

You are forewarned. Be prepared. No big deal so long as you have a backup copy of your speech with you!

Lessons Learned

- If a teleprompter is used for your speech, it can keep you on time and on track for the message.
- Training on proper use of a teleprompter is needed.
- Don't mimic a metronome with your head and eyes moving back and forth from one screen to the other. Mix it up and lob a look to center and back to the screen you just left.
- Anticipate teleprompter problems, such as the wrong speech being displayed or failure of equipment. Have a paper copy of the speech on the podium or in your pocket!
- Practice, practice, and practice until you feel comfortable, not when the teleprompter operator says no more practice is needed. It is your speech!
- Look at specific individuals in the audience in different areas of room to deliver a speech in which they believe you are talking directly to them.

Chapter 19

ALL GOOD THINGS MUST COME TO AN END

Be not sad when the end is here; rejoice for the seeds planted in fertile soil. Your words live on.

—Donald J. Palmisano

The end of a speech is the closing message, the ask of the audience. It is what the body of your speech has been building toward and it will be the final impression of you and your speech.

It is imperative to capture the audience within the first thirty seconds of your speech, but it is equally important not to lose them at the end. Just as people remember the first time they met you, they also remember when you parted company.

The end should be planned carefully:

1. A brief summary of the presentation, such as the three key points
2. A reference to a powerful, emotional story told in the body of the speech and tied to the overall message of your speech
3. The ask of the audience, that is, what you hope they will do
4. The thanks to the audience for their time and attention

Don't end a speech by rushing through the last part because you did not stay on your timed outline and, instead, wandered into other comments outside of your practiced delivery. You don't want to look disorganized at the conclusion of your speech because you did not follow a disciplined pace.

If you told a powerful story, refer to it as part of your ending. You hope they will carry "Little Johnny's" story with them always and work to change things so no other child suffers that fate. If you tie a powerful story into your conclusion, neither you nor the story will be forgotten.

Lessons Learned

- The end of a speech is the final message, the ask of the audience.
- It is imperative that you capture the audience within the first thirty seconds, but it is equally important that you do not lose them at the end.
- The end should be planned carefully with a brief summary of the presentation—that is, the three key points, a reference to the powerful, emotional story told in the speech, the ask of the audience, the thank you, and then end.
- Don't end a speech by rushing through the last part because you did not stay on your timed outline.
- Never forget that people remember stories!

Chapter 20

EQUIPMENT FOR PRACTICING SPEECHES AND RECORDING FOR SOCIAL MEDIA

Gadgets intrigue me, especially recorders and cameras. They freeze moments in time for future generations. The memory lives on.

—Donald J. Palmisano

I always emphasize practicing your speech many times before the day of the actual speech. The best way to get the most out of the practice is to record yourself.

Watch the video after each delivery of the speech and note things you want to change. Perhaps you unconsciously look down too much or maybe you avert your eyes to the ceiling. Listen for whether you smack your lips. Listen for "you know" or "ahh" during pauses. These undesirable actions usually are done without your awareness, and you have no knowledge of them until viewed on the video. Seeing these actions on the video usually leads to the disappearance of these tic-like activities.

The equipment for the practice sessions can be inexpensive. A tripod to hold a phone that records video will work. Though a willing friend with a steady hand can work as a substitute. I use an enhanced recording and viewing system for teaching the third- and fourth-year medical students at Tulane University School of Medicine. Each student does a two-minute speech on any topic and then does a self-critique of the performance after viewing. Five other students then critique the performance and then I also critique it. We all learn from each other! Remember, the journey to a standing ovation includes practice, practice, practice!

Components of DJP's Video and Audio Recording Setup

Here are the components of my setup for teaching students at Tulane University School of Medicine and for my own practice prior to keynote speeches:

1. **Video camera:** Canon VIXIA HF R500. It contains an audio input jack, which is significant because the audio recorded with the camera's internal microphone is never as good as an external microphone. It is important to buy a video camera that has an audio input jack. Some expensive cameras do not. I bought this camera after it was out of production by Canon, but I wanted it because of the audio jack. I found it new on Amazon for $200.00. Although this one is no longer available on Amazon, you can get the Canon Vixia HF R800 for $200 as of August 2019. It also has an audio input or microphone jack and reviewers state you need a powered microphone to connect into it. The AZDEN microphone I use and describe below is a powered microphone (uses 9-volt batteries in transmitter and receiver).

2. **Tripod:** Alta Pro 263AT. This tripod that I use for my flower macrophotography works well, but you can get a less expensive tripod for the recording session. This Alta Pro cost around $150 several years ago. Less costly tripods that will work for this purpose are available for around $20 on Amazon. The video camera attaches to the tripod. A rubber loop clip can be used to hold the

audio receiver to the tripod after the connection is made to the audio input.

3. **Microphone:** AZDEN WMS-PRO VHF Wireless Microphone System. It includes a lavalier clip-on electret condenser microphone and a receiver plus an alternate handheld electret condenser microphone. The receiver connects to the audio input of the camera. I have used this same piece of equipment for many years. It is reliable. As of August 2019, it is available on Amazon for about $150.

4. **TV Screen:** 18.5-inch screen (diagonal) Samsung (720 p), model UN19F4000AF. I purchased it at Best Buy and it weighs 5.7 pounds with the stand. The important point to remember is to get a screen that has a USB input on the back so you can load the SD card into a USB card reader and connect to the TV. This model has USB input and also has two HDMI jacks on back. This model has software inside the TV that allows you to play the video without difficulty. Simple and efficient. The cost of the TV some years ago was about $150.

5. Alternatively, you can play back the SD recording flash drive from the video camera by using your computer. For my teaching sessions, I play back the student's speech on the Samsung TV screen. Innovations in the future may use different input systems into the viewing screen. The important point is for you to have a system that allows what you record to be viewed immediately on a larger screen than the camera's small playback screen.

6. **Podium:** I use a Gleam Sheet music stand as a podium substitute during practice sessions. It is lightweight and comes with a carrying case. I bought it on Amazon in March 2019 for $30. It functions well, collapses easily, and has 4.8 stars out of 5 on Amazon.

7. **Timer:** You must be aware of the length of time of your speech and how much time is left as you are delivering

the speech. It is best not to keep glancing at a wristwatch. Looking at a watch on your wrist causes the audience to think you want to get out of the auditorium. Better to have a timer on the podium with you. I recommend you bring your own timer as you have control of the type of timer and you know how to use it. It should have a large enough face to easily show the time left. The type of timer I find most helpful is a timer that shows in large numbers the time left as well as the time you have been talking. My favorite is the "Marathon DualTimer with Large Display, Magnetic Back and Stand." It measures 4.8 x 4.1 x 1.5 inches, large enough to see easily and small enough to carry without difficulty. You have the option of setting an alarm on the timer with three different volume intensities. I got my timer from Amazon in April 2019 for $20.

8. Placing your watch on the podium carries the risk of losing the watch. I have lost two watches over the years. Frequently at the end of the speech people will come to the podium to ask additional questions beyond the questions handled in the Q and A portion of your talk. The watch can be forgotten or knocked off as you pick up your notes to meet the questioners. I strongly recommend you don't put your watch on the podium. Unfortunately, no one had returned my lost watches to lost and found when I inquired.

My complete system described above has worked well for years. As the years go by, the equipment mentioned no doubt will be replaced by newer models or equipment not yet imagined. The point is to use something to record yourself so you can get an idea of how the audience hears and sees you. That is how you learn and improve.

But remember, you can start your practice with any phone that records high-quality video. You will need a tripod and a clamp device to secure the phone and aim it at you. Or you may be able to get a clamp for the phone and attach it to something in your home or office. Amazon sells various brands of clamp devices for iPhones and other smart phones.

If you desire to record just your voice in a practice session, most smartphones come with voice recording options or you could invest in an excellent small recorder, the Sony ICD-UX560. It is 0.43 inches thick and records in .MP3 or .WAV format. For practice sessions, the .MP3 format is fine and takes up less space on the 4GB internal hard drive or the optional microSD card. It recharges via a built-in pop-out USB. Battery life is twenty-seven hours. You also can attach a Sony lavalier microphone to the 3.5mm audio input jack. I found it to be excellent for practicing speeches and for recording interviews. It has great reviews.[1]

I tend to use Amazon as an easy way to check out equipment, but other stores such as Best Buy will work as well. If a local recording or camera store is available to you, try them first. The advice in the local, dedicated stores is often invaluable.

Equipment for Self-Recording for Social Media

If you are self-recording a video to put on social media such as YouTube, be certain to have the highest quality microphone and recording camera you can afford. Without getting into the specifics of all of the available brands, the goal is to purchase equipment that will give you the sound quality of National Public Radio (NPR). In addition, it is essential that you are framed properly in the video. Poor framing of the person speaking and poor audio quality are the telltale signs of a nonprofessional. Accurate framing and volume are especially important if you are recording on a phone, as is often easiest.

1. **Microphone:** You will have to decide if you are going to use a microphone that uses a 3.5mm jack connection

or the higher quality 3-pin XLR connection. The XLR option has additional advantages, such as protection against electrical interference and availability of "phantom power" that some microphones require. Without getting into any more technicalities, do some test recordings with the system you plan to use and listen with headphones to determine if the quality you desire is present.

I always record in a high-quality format such as .WAV or another lossless format for my master recording. You can always reduce to a smaller format of lesser quality, but you cannot upgrade a lesser quality recorded format to a higher quality. The higher quality format easily can be converted to the compressed .MP3 if the social media platform you are seeking accepts only .MP3. Some believe .MP3, which samples the sound and has a smaller file, is adequate for voices but .WAV is essential for music as it captures all of the sound.

2. **Recording Device:** I use the Tascam DR-44WL Four-Track Recorder with Stereo Microphones built-in, XLR Microphone Inputs for two additional microphones, and Wi-Fi. I connect two lavalier XLR microphones (Audio Technica AT899) to the XLR inputs when I am interviewing someone for my DJP Update Enhanced Podcasts (a.k.a. my vlog).[2] My interviewee wears one and I wear the other. The Tascam is small, portable, and does a great job in .WAV or .MP3.

Another less expensive and portable option is the small Sony ICD-ux560 mentioned earlier that records in .WAV (listed on the machine as LPCM) or .MP3. I use the Sony lavalier microphone ECMCS3 Clip-Style Omnidirectional Stereo with it, but the recorder doesn't have XLR input. It only has one input. So if you want to record another person and yourself with two lavalier microphones, you need two recorders and then you have to mix the voices later in post-production. You can use just one microphone, but then both voices may sound distant or one will be distant if one person has the lavalier microphone and the second person is farther from the microphone. To make sure the sound of the voices matches with the lips moving, it is important to use a clapboard or clap your hands at the start of the interview so that that loud sound can be synchronized during the mixing of the sound and the video. Of course, you can avoid the last step by connecting the microphone jack into the audio input of a camera that records video. Then everything is in sync. But remember, not all cameras have an audio input. Look for it when considering the purchase of a camera.

In my opinion, Curtis Judd has excellent videos on YouTube explaining recording equipment and more. [3]

After recording, you can use editing software to create a professional appearance and sound. Examples of video editing software for beginners include iMovie, Wondershare's Filmora, and Windows Movie Maker. Ready, set, post your video!

So, why go to this extra effort in practicing and recording your speech repeatedly? Because you want to do very well! The world has heard enough of mediocrity. When a true orator arises in their midst, they will stand up and applaud. Go for it.

To be a great orator you don't have to be born with a body that makes you a star athlete or have a face that advertisers want to put in TV ads. You just have to have a message that you present with style, using techniques proven over centuries and amplified by a compelling personal story told with passion. You just have to practice and record your message to give you feedback on your performance and help you enhance your style of delivery. You just have to do your homework, have courage, and don't give up!

Lessons Learned

- Practice your speech many times before the day of the speech.
- The best way to get the most out of the practice is to record yourself.
- Review the sample audio and video system described above to record your speech and consider the use of a podium and timer.
- As the years go by the recording equipment will change, but the goal remains the same: record your speech and review the recording so you can improve your performance.
- If you post videos on social media, choose your equipment wisely and strive for the sound quality of NPR. And don't forget that the proper framing of your image is equally important.
- After recording, use editing software readily available to achieve a professional standard video.

Chapter 21

CAMERA-READY: LOOKING YOUR PERSONAL BEST

Clothes make the man. Naked people have little or no influence on society.

—Mark Twain

The first impression the audience gets of you is how you look when you walk out on the stage. Your choice of clothing and grooming makes a strong, nonverbal statement to the audience. The second impression is how you handle the first moments of your speech, discussed in Chapter 1.

Your goal is to score high with both of these impressions. Doing so will prime the audience to be more receptive to the message in your speech.

The audience will evaluate your personal appearance on a number of factors, but a failure in any one of them can deflate their impression, just as a balloon deflates with one pin hole.

Clothing

You should dress appropriately for the occasion. For a business convention, women would fit in with a tailored dress, a skirt or suit, or similar business attire. A suit is the traditional business attire for men, but a sports jacket with a tailored pair of pants might suffice. For men, a suit in a solid color without flashy patterns is usually the safest choice.

Avoid wearing small checkered patterns because digital sensors may create moiré, a pattern that is distorting. Avoidance of such a patterned fabric in clothing is especially important if appearing before television or other video cameras.

The next question for men is whether to wear a tie with the suit or sports jacket. The safest choice is a tie, however, I note an increase in male speakers who wear a dress shirt unbuttoned at the neck and no tie. Also, some speakers feel comfortable presenting in a turtleneck or even a round or V-neck T-shirt. Best to err on the majority side and wear a tie if in doubt.

In 2019, I received the National Association of Corporate Directors (NACD) designation of NACD Board Leadership Fellow as a result of attending multiple courses and lectures. The lectures consisted of a wide range of speakers over the years. Some creative entrepreneurs did not wear a suit, but instead walked out on stage in jeans and a T-shirt. For those individuals, that style of dress was appropriate. You only have to view some YouTube videos or Apple videos of Steve Jobs on stage in his black turtleneck shirt at a new product announcement to realize some speakers do it their own way because they are trailblazers and know the visionary product will trump the dress attire, but not every speaker can pull off the business-casual wear that Silicon Valley has popularized.

Sometimes the conference at which you are speaking is a retreat for the attendees and everyone, including those speaking, is expected to dress in a more business-casual fashion. You should check the conference brochure or reach out to the meeting contact person if the proper attire is not clear to you because you do not want your clothes to be an item of discussion by being inappropriate for the dress code of the meeting.

One very important styling concept my wife, Robin, taught me is to choose clothing in colors that brighten your appearance. After marrying Robin, my attire changed. One day I came home from making rounds at the hospital and noted my clothes locker was missing half of my suits. She had given them to Goodwill! My wife explained I am a "Winter" and should not be wearing warm-toned brown and beige jackets or suits. She taught me a "Winter" should wear cooler tones of navy, gray, or black in suits and jackets and, if warmer tones of brown or beige are necessary for some reason, that I should wear a complimentary colored shirt near my face.

As Robin explained, the concept is "seasonal color analysis" and the goal is to determine the palette of colors that best harmonize with your natural coloring. At the core of seasonal color analysis is the theory that the combination of skin, eyes, and hair color determines what range of colors you wear best.[1]

Ideally, you should have a person knowledgeable in the topic of personal styling advise you regarding your best colors, fit, and all other aspects of looking your personal best. More information about wardrobe color palettes for your best look can be found on the Internet.[2] Doing a color analysis for your best attire is a worthwhile investment for improving your standing ovation speech!

Hair, Makeup, and Eyewear

A speaker's hair should be trimmed and styled appropriately. Make certain its length or style does not cover the eyes or otherwise diminish your facial expression while speaking. Facial expression is key to connecting with your audience.

Men take notice: unless you are a genius presenting the equivalent of a formula stating energy is equal to the mass multiplied by the speed of light squared ($E = MC^2$), you should avoid untrimmed hair on your head, an unruly beard, hair projecting out of your nostrils and ears, and hair sprouting like weeds down the back of your neck. Don't allow such distractions in your appearance.

Makeup is a personal choice but, if chosen, wear it wisely.

While perhaps not as important before a live audience, makeup is essential to look your best on television or video. If you are unfamiliar with the application of makeup, I recommend you seek consultation with an expert who can organize a portable makeup kit and guide you on a few basics of application or review some of the many available makeup tutorials online.

At a minimum, it is important you address the moisture or oil on the face that creates a shiny appearance when the lights focus on you. This is particularly true before the high definition lens cameras of a television studio. If you are in a major TV studio, there usually is a makeup artist who will eliminate shine on your face and otherwise apply makeup to the degree you are comfortable, but someone else may use up the available time with the station's makeup artist and, in smaller TV studios, a makeup artist is rarely available. So you should have a backup plan in place.

It helps to limit the shine if you wash your face just before the presentation or interview and then apply a powder gel that dries quickly. Lancôme® T-Zone is what my wife taught me to use, but I recently discovered it is no longer on the market. Check with a makeup consultant to determine a Lancôme® T-Zone equivalent for a portable, quick fix to the facial shine you want to avoid when the bright lights hit.

If you wear glasses and need them for the presentation or interview, get the antireflective coating applied to the glasses so people can see your eyes and not the light reflections on the glasses. You don't want the audience distracted. Also, have a spare pair of eyeglasses if needed to read text. Glasses come apart at the most inconvenient times!

Unique Concerns for Appearance before Television or Video Cameras

Speaking on television or before a video recording device requires unique appearance considerations of how you are coming across to an audience you cannot see. It is always important to look at the person or persons you are addressing, but you must understand the difference between speaking before a live audience, a televised interview in-studio, a televised interview from a remote location, and a video recording device.

With a live audience, you should maintain eye contact by moving your eyes from one group of individuals in the audience to another group. It is a more natural form of audience interaction.

If you are speaking before television cameras on-set with an anchor or host conducting the interview, you should look at the camera with the red light illuminated on top when you are introduced. After the introduction, you keep your eyes on the person interviewing you. The interaction becomes a conversation that the audience is observing.

If you are before a television camera in a remote recording studio that is transmitting the recording live to the national television station, you are not in the same room as the person interviewing you. The audience can no longer observe a conversation between you and the interviewer seated together and looking at one another but, instead, will see you and the interviewer at separate times on-screen or, perhaps, at the same time if a split screen presentation is utilized.

In the remote recording studio environment, always look at the camera directly in front of you. *Do not* look to the side where there is a TV monitor showing what the viewing audience is seeing, that is, either the interviewer or you. If you look at the side TV monitor, the audience will see you looking to the side instead of directly into the recording camera and will think you are nervous, shifty-eyed, or not telling the truth. Also, there may be a slight lag in appearance on the TV monitor which may confuse you. When I am in a remote studio, I ask the person who is filming me to put a cover or sheet over the TV monitor so I will not be tempted to look. You always want to be looking directly into the camera.

Whether being interviewed in-studio or from a remote location for a television program with more than one person hosting the show, always ask who will be interviewing you. Sometimes they will say person A, and then person B conducts the interview. If you are in a remote studio and take my advice about never looking at the TV monitor placed to your side, you will not see the interviewer to confirm that the person conducting the interview is who you expected. So if you don't recognize the voice of the person asking the question, don't guess at the name in the response. Just say, "Thanks for having me on the show and the answer to your question is . . ."

If speaking before a video recording device, the principle of looking directly into the camera still applies. If you are self-recording your speech or other form of presentation to place on social media, you don't want to be difficult to hear or sound like you are in an echo chamber. You want to use the best quality recording equipment that is within your budget. I have a few suggestions of what you might consider in Chapter 20.

Finally, if presenting in a television or other recording studio, or even if your speech before a live audience is being recorded, be certain to request a copy of your televised segment or video recording. Most will accommodate you. Alternatively, if on television, be certain to arrange ahead of time for your interview or other presentation to be recorded on a home device.

Name Tags

Often you are given a name tag when you are invited to be a speaker at a meeting. The trend is for the name tag to be on a lanyard. While perhaps intended to avoid damage to the material of your shirt or suit that may occur by clipping or pinning a name tag, the lanyard is not ideal because half of the lanyards on people are flipped around and the name of the person is not apparent. Your name always should be in view because you want everyone to connect your name with your face and your brilliant ideas rather than to walk away wondering, "Who is that person?"

Think of how you might stabilize the lanyard so that your name is showing, perhaps by adding the extra weight of meal tickets or a hotel key placed in the plastic holder behind your name. If the plastic name cover attached to the lanyard has a clip or pin on the back of it, consider removing the name tag from the lanyard and simply attaching the name tag to your shirt or suit jacket. When attaching the name tag to your shirt or suit jacket, place it on your right side. If placed on the left, the person walking up to you is forced to look to their right to read your name and it becomes apparent that person does not know your name or has forgotten. It is a courtesy to them to allow them to look at your right hand to shake and then as their eyes move up to the level of your eyes, they will see your name in a natural flow.

One more important tip about name tags. Take off the name tag when you get on the stage to speak. Why? Because the professional photographers frequently use flash to photograph you while speaking and the flash bounces off of the name tag. Small detail, but again the professional touch. Obviously, you want the best image taken of you during a memorable speech. With a light bounce of the flash off of a tag, the photo editor may reject the image for any publication planned.

Additional Appearance Tips

Avoid eating just before speaking as it may make you less alert and also you may get food stuck in between your teeth! You don't want to be moving your tongue to try to dislodge lettuce or a piece of meat when you should be talking. Again, no distractions for the audience.

Apply balm, such as ChapStick® or lipstick, to your lips to prevent the sensation of dryness caused by the adrenaline release commonly associated with the excitement of public speaking.

Otherwise, you will lick your lips repeatedly without awareness. Watch enough televised news and you will see less experienced, on-camera speakers doing it to the detriment of their message.

Stand up straight when presenting. Don't bend your neck down at the podium, read your notes, and mumble! You want eye contact with the audience. It is permissible to glance at notes, but you want to engage the audience with your eyes.

If you wear hearing aids, put in new batteries, or charge the rechargeable models prior to the presentation. You don't want that beeping noise in your ears informing you the batteries are dying. You don't need distractions and you need to hear.

If you have other disabilities, tell the organizers of the event what you need to be comfortable on the stage. If in a wheelchair or using crutches, point out what works best for you. Don't try to adapt yourself to the standard stage, let them adapt conditions to suit you. Take charge and give your requests to them. You want to give full attention to your speech and not be impeded by uncomfortable conditions. It always helps to have a "handler," someone on your team who can take care of these issues and get you to the correct location timely. Dr. Juan Watkins of Shreveport, Louisiana, was my "handler" when I ran for the board and later the office of president of the American Medical Association and he is the best handler I have ever seen.

Whenever and wherever you are speaking, don't forget to smile! Be likeable, or your message may be rejected by the audience.

Lessons Learned

- Audiences form impressions of you when you walk on stage. First, how you dress and groom, as well as what you say in the first thirty seconds.
- Attire should be appropriate for the occasion.

- Proper grooming of hair is important, including trimming hair in your ears and nose.
- Determine your best clothing colors using seasonal color analysis (i.e., Summer, Autumn, Winter, and Spring) based on the color of your skin, eyes, and hair.
- Use makeup to get rid of shine on your face.
- If you wear eyeglasses, use antireflective lenses with an extra pair available in case of breakage.
- Remember the importance of looking at the person or persons you are speaking to and the adaptation you must make if before a live audience, a televised interview in-studio, a televised interview from a remote location, and a video recording device.
- Always look into the camera when in a remote location from the main studio and not at the TV monitor on the side.
- Don't eat immediately before speaking.
- Apply balm, such as ChapStick® or lipstick, before speaking.
- Make certain your name tag is showing when mingling with the audience, but remove your name tag before your speech.
- Maintain good posture.
- If you wear hearing aids, always carry fresh batteries.
- Smile!

Chapter 22

THE EVER-READY TWO-MINUTE SPEECH ABOUT YOU

The best extemporaneous speech is the one well-prepared.
—Attorney Jessie McDonald of Monroe, Louisiana,
1975, as told to Donald J. Palmisano

When running for the American Medical Association (AMA) Board of Trustees and later for the presidency of AMA, the other candidates and I were allowed only two minutes to present our speech to the 550 (now over 600) voting delegates from across the United States. Having only two minutes to sell yourself as the best candidate for the position requires that you efficiently accentuate the key points of your message because failing to stay within the two-minute time frame may cost you the election.

Everyone should write a two-minute speech explaining why she or he should be selected for a job, residency, clerkship, or elective office. A powerful two-minute speech detailing personal qualifications and why you should be selected is more difficult that a thirty-minute speech. It must be concise, yet pertinent in each section of the speech.

The ideal is to have a short personal story included that moves the listener to gain important insight into your character and motivation. Also, within that two-minute time frame, you should speak not only of your qualifications for the positon, but also inspire the listener by explaining with passion what your plan is to solve the problems of the organization and strengthen its viability for years to come.

I include the short story of my failure of the first exam in gross anatomy at Tulane Medical School. I was convinced I was not smart enough to be a doctor and told my dad I was quitting medical school. His immediate response was, "Why would you do that? You are smart enough to be a doctor. Do the following and you will succeed: do your homework, have courage, and don't give up! Do those three things and nothing in life is impossible."

I followed his advice and graduated with honors from Tulane Medical School. The person listening to me gains insight about me as a person and appreciates the wisdom of that advice. Without my policeman father as my mentor, my life would be very different.

Be prepared to include in your two-minute speech why you want the position at the organization, such as a surgical resident, law firm associate, federal court clerk, software engineer, or publishing company editor.

It is not easy to concisely include personal background information and career goals, but with work you can do it. Most people don't take the time to prepare in this fashion and, therefore, you will stand out from your competitors for the position.

Next, you have to be prepared to answer five questions:

1. What is your strongest point for this position or job?
2. What is your weakest point for this position or job?
3. What do you like best about our residency (or company, organization, etc.)?
4. Do you have a hobby? If so, what is it?
5. What is your greatest success to date and also your greatest failure?

I remember vividly asking question number two, the weakest point, to a bright, articulate doctor running for an elective position on a council of the American Medical Association. He froze and could not give a response. He was not elected. Years later, I was teaching a course in the Cayman Islands and he happened to be on the island on holiday. He walked up to me and said my question had destroyed him. He did not know how to respond. I told him I was sorry for his disappointment, but that is a standard question I ask of candidates. The response tells a lot about the candidate.

So, be prepared! Do your homework and work on your two-minute speech. Practice it many times so that you have it memorized, yet it flows out of you as regular conversation. Only practice can make your answer flow easily. You are forewarned. Act accordingly. Success requires preparation and the courage to act.

Lessons Learned

- The best speech is the one well prepared.
- Write a two-minute speech about yourself that can be used for any interview situation. The essence of your qualifications and your vision for the job, residency, clerkship, or elected office should be condensed into two-minutes for the initial interview or campaign speech. It can be expanded at the listeners' request.
- Within that two-minute time frame, you should speak not only of your qualifications for the position but also inspire the listener by explaining with passion what your plan is to solve the problems of the organization and strengthen its viability for years to come.
- Anticipate questions from the interviewer or audience. What are your strong points? Your weak points? Why is your message important? What are your hobbies? Practice the responses and anticipate questions.

- What would you ask someone applying for a job or other position? Be prepared to answer those questions about yourself.
- And don't forget to smile!

Chapter 23

HOW TO GET AN INVITATION TO SPEAK

Small opportunities are often the beginning of great enterprises.

—Demosthenes

You have studied the advice in this book. You have written a speech. You have practiced the speech repeatedly. Now it's showtime! But how do you get an invitation to speak?

One way is to publish in professional journals related to your career. Another is to write an op-ed on the subject of your speech and secure its publication in a local or national newspaper. Look for opportunities to publish in popular magazines. Call your hometown radio and television stations and ask if they will invite you on to discuss the important topic you would like to present in a speech. A published article or op-ed, or speaking on radio or television, can expose you to people who would otherwise be unfamiliar with you and lead to speech invitations.

If you are a member of a professional organization, explore speaking opportunities within that organization. Professional organizations that offer continuing education for licensure requirements are always looking for speakers and, if you deliver a good speech, additional speaking invitations from those in the audience likely will ensue.

If you are in a profession that holds meetings to debate positions on professional ethics or proposed laws that will affect the profession, go to a state or national meeting of the organization and try to speak at the microphone during the debate of a topic. For example, doctors who belong to their state medical association or the AMA can work to be a delegate to the meeting with microphone privileges. Even if you are not a delegate, you can speak at reference committees evaluating a resolution before it goes to the full debate in the House of Delegates. If you present a two-minute comment pertinent to the topic under discussion in an organized, polite, and logical, yet passionate, manner, you may impress others and invitations to speak on the topic at their local or state meetings may follow.

To gain practice in speaking publicly, look into local service organizations such as the Rotary Club, Junior League, or Friends of the Library, which may offer speaking opportunities in addition to the opportunity of contributing to the welfare of the community. Such service organizations, plus neighborhood associations and social clubs, may provide a venue for public speaking opportunities that lead to more professionally robust invitations to speak.

And don't forget the possibility of social media, including Twitter, Facebook, YouTube, and others available now and those to be created in the future. Stay up to date for ways to introduce your message. Sharing your message and style of speaking can lead to invitations. Be creative in your thinking and use editing software readily available to make a profession video.

I suggest reading: *New Think* by Edward de Bono and *A Whack on the Side of the Head* by Dr. Roger von Oech. Those books are good stimuli for creativity. If nothing develops from those examples, put together a wonderful speech and create a free YouTube channel. Post the speech and spread the word on Twitter that your comments are available on YouTube. Alert friends to retweet. One caution: the famous advertising man, William Bernbach, said in a *Wall Street Journal* interview, "Great advertising can make a bad product fail faster; it gets more people to know it's bad."[1]

Lessons Learned

- To get speech invitations, publish in professional journals and popular magazines on your speech topic, write an op-ed on the subject of your speech and get it published in a local or national newspaper, call your hometown radio and television stations and ask if they will invite you on to discuss the important topic.
- If you are a member of a professional organization, explore speaking opportunities within the organization. Also, go to its local or national meetings and speak at the microphone during the debate of a topic.
- Join local service, neighborhood, or social organizations and take advantage of opportunities to speak publicly before the membership.
- Communicate your views on social media, including Twitter, Facebook, and YouTube.
- Read creative thinking books to expand your ideas for speaking opportunities. Consider *New Think* and *A Whack on the Side of the Head*.
- Do your homework on the speech and be prepared for questions. You only get one chance to make a good first impression. Remember Bernbach's observation, "Great advertising can make a bad product fail faster; it gets more people to know it's bad."

NOTES

Introduction: Why Another Book on Speeches?

1. Donald J. Palmisano at National Press Club, July 9, 2003. https: //www.npr.org/programs/npc/2003/030709.dpalmisano.html (Accessed October 18, 2019).
2. Donald J. Palmisano, *"Medicine: A Noble Profession,"* *Vital Speeches of the Day,* September 15, 2002.
3. Donald J. Palmisano, *"Advice from the Past—Hope for the Future,"* *Vital Speeches of the Day,* August 15, 2003.
4. Donald J. Palmisano, "Leadership in Public Health," *Vital Speeches of the Day,* November 10, 2003.
5. Donald J. Palmisano, "Medical Leadership<em-dash>United We Triumph, Divided We Fail," *Vital Speeches of the Day,* January 1, 2004.
6. Donald J. Palmisano, Chicago Council speech on *Leadership in Public Health* also was published in *Executive Speeches,* Dec. 2003–Jan. 2004.
7. Donald J. Palmisano, "Why Your Doctor Might Quit," *Saturday Evening Post.* Nov.–Dec. 2004; No. 6, Vol. 276; Pg. 50.

Chapter 1: Panic!

1. https://www.therichest.com/luxury/most-expensive/10-most -expensive-mens-suits-in-the-world/ (Accessed July 1, 2019).
2. https://www.armani.com/us/armanicom/giorgio-armani/men/all -clothing (Accessed July 1, 2019).
3. https://intrepidresources.com/html/risk.html (Accessed July 22, 2019).
4. https://archive.org/details/50564TheMagneticRecorder (Accessed October 2, 2019).

Chapter 2: The Four Key Elements of a Memorable Speech

1. https://www.facebook.com/goalcast/videos/rocky-motivational -speech/958676217542902/ (Accessed November 7, 2019).

2.   https://www.forbes.com/sites/nickmorgan/2014/12/23/why-is-passion
-important-in-public-speaking/#748fa80855dd (Accessed November 10,
2019)

3.   Thomas Montalbo, *The Power of Eloquence, Prentice-Hall* in Englewood
Cliffs, N.J. 1984—Library of Congress PN4121 .M584 1984; SBN 10–
0136876579, 0136876404.

Chapter 3: Aristotle's Rhetoric

1.   https://blog.ed.ted.com/2017/01/17/rhetoric-101-the-art-of
-persuasive-speech/ (Accessed November 7, 2019*)*.

2.   See note 1 above.

3.   Shraddha Bajracharya, "Aristotle's Model of Communication," in *Businesstopia*,
January 6, 2018. https://www.businesstopia.net/communication/aristotles-
model-communication. (Accessed July 29, 2019).

4.   https://blog.ed.ted.com/2017/01/17/rhetoric-101-the-art-of
-persuasive-speech/ (Accessed July 29, 2019).

Chapter 4: Learn from Leading Advocates, Now and in the Past

1.   https://www2.stetson.edu/advocacy-journal/a-grave-responsibility-a
-rhetorical-critique-of-the-opening-statement-at-nuremberg-using-the
-narrative-perspective/ (Accessed August 11, 2019).

2.   http://www.abajournal.com/magazine/article/powerful_eloquence
_justice_robert_jackson (Accessed August 11, 2019).

3.   Palmisano, Donald J. *The Little Red Book of Leadership Lessons* (Little Red
Books). (New York: Skyhorse Publishing. Kindle Edition. 2011).

4.   https://teachingamericanhistory.org/library/document/report
-on-the-nuremberg-trials/ and https://crimeofaggression.info/documents
/6/1946_Nuremberg_Judgement.pdf (Accessed November 9, 2019).

5.   https://www.roberthjackson.org/about/ (Accessed August 11, 2019).

6.   https://thejacksonlist.com (Accessed August 11, 2019).

7.   https://www.roberthjackson.org/speech-and-writing/justice-jacksons
-final-report/ (Accessed August 12, 2019).

8.   https://www.cov.com/en/professionals/h/philip-howard (Accessed October
5, 2019).

9.   https://intrepidresources.com/djp_update/?cat=175 (Accessed October
5, 2019).

10. https://www.forbes.com/sites/steveforbes/2019/08/26/can-a-return
-to-common-sense-save-our-democracy-philip-howard/#4fde8f5431bb
(Accessed August 29, 2019).

11. http://www.faucheux.com (Accessed October 5, 2019).

12. https://www.triallawyerportraits.org/russ-herman (Accessed August
28, 2019).

13. https://www.publicjustice.net/attorney-russ-herman-to-receive-2019
-champion-of-justice-award/ (Accessed October 5, 2019).
14. https://www.publicjustice.net/attorney-russ-herman-to-receive-2019
-champion-of-justice-award/ (Accessed October 5, 2019).

Chapter 5: A Speechwriter's Playbook
1. https://www.linkedin.com/in/robert-friedman-678066135 (Accessed October 5, 2019).
2. See note 1 above.
3. https://www.dermrounds.com/profiles/blogs/dr-george-hruza-delivers
-inspirational-speech-at-the-aad-plenary- (Accessed October 5, 2019).

Chapter 6: The Speechwriter's Toolbox
1. William Strunk Jr., and E. B. White, The Elements of Style, 3rd ed. (New York: Allyn and Bacon, 1979), 23.
2. E. B. White, *Here is New York* (New York: Harper & Row, Publishers, Inc. 1977), 132. Permission granted for quote.
3. Lucile Vaughan Payne, *The Lively Art of Writing*, (Chicago: Follett Publishing Company, 1965).
4. Marie L. Waddell, Robert M. Esch, and Roberta R. Walker, *The Art of Styling Sentences: 20 Patterns to Success*, (New York: Barron's Educational Series, Inc., 1972).
5. Stephen King, *On Writing – A Memoir of the Craft*, (New York: Scribner, 2000).
6. https://www.stephenking.com and https://en.wikipedia.org/wiki/Stephen_King accessed August 20, 2019).
7. Dean Koontz, *How to Write Best Selling Fiction* (Cincinnati, Ohio: Writers Digest Books, 1981).
8. https://www.deankoontz.com/about-dean (Accessed October 4, 2019).
9. John Hough Jr., *The Fiction Writer's Guide to Dialogue* (New York, Skyhorse Publishing, 2015).
10 William Zinsser, *On Writing Well* (New York: Harper & Row, 1976).
11. David Rattray (Editor) and staff in association with Peter Davies, *Reader's Digest Success With Words* (New York: The Reader's Digest Association, 1983).
12. Frank N. McGill, *Magill's Quotations in Context Second Series* (New York: Harper & Row, 1969).
13. https://www.thegreatcourses.com (Accessed November 10, 2019).

Chapter 7: Libraries as a Resource
1. https://librarytechnology.org/library/199689 (Accessed October 5, 2019).

2. https://www.gatesfoundation.org/Media-Center/Press-Releases/1997/06/Bill-and-Melinda-Gates-Establish-Library-Foundation (Accessed October 5, 2019).
3. http://www.loc.gov/pictures/ (Accessed October 5, 2019).
4. https://www.loc.gov/item/2017806114/ (Accessed October 5, 2019).
5. https://www.loc.gov/item/2017762891/ (Accessed October 5, 2019).
6. https://www.loc.gov/collections/fsa-owi-black-and-white-negatives/about-this-collection/ (Accessed October 5, 2019).
7. Frank Billings, "Pernicious Anemia." *Journal of the American Medical Association*, Vol. XXXVII No. 9, (1901): 577-581.

Chapter 8: Rhetorical Devices Make Speech Soar

1. The King James version of the Bible uses "every thing" as opposed to "everything".
2. https://examples.yourdictionary.com/alliteration-examples.html (Accessed October 2, 2019).
3. https://en.wikipedia.org/wiki/William_Lloyd_Garrison (Accessed October 2, 2019).
4. https://www.americanrhetoric.com (Accessed October 2, 2019).
5. Richard Greene, and Florie Brizel, *Words That Shook The World,* (New York: Prentice Hall Press, 2002).
6. https://www.thoughtco.com/rhetorical-devices-4169905 (Accessed August 19, 2019).
7. https://examples.yourdictionary.com/examples-of-rhetorical-devices.html (Accessed August 19, 2019).

Chapter 9: In the Beginning

1. Autobiographical dictation, 11 October 1907. Published in *Autobiography of Mark Twain, Vol. 3* (University of California Press, 2015). See https://patriciachubb.com/pause-for-a-quote-by-mark-twain (Accessed October 16, 2019).
2. https://www.warhistoryonline.com/war-articles/the-best-quotes-lines-from-the-longest-day.html (Accessed July 24, 2019) and Donald Palmisano, *On Leadership* (New York: Skyhorse Publishing, 2008).
3. http://libguides.merrimack.edu/research_help/Sources (Accessed July 28, 2019).
4. Donald J. Palmisano, *The Six Commandments of Medicine* https://intrepidresources.com/html/commencement_address.pdf (Accessed October 18, 2019).
5. https://www.genardmethod.com/blog/bid/142073/how-to-start-a-speech-12-foolproof-ways-to-grab-your-audience (Accessed July 24, 2019).
6. Donald J. Palmisano, Nuremberg Legacy. https://www.youtube.com/watch?v=JWj1zOBi_Uo (Accessed August 12, 2019).

7. Irving Younger's *10 Commandments of Cross Examination* https://www
.youtube.com/watch?v=dBP2if0l-a8 (Accessed November 6, 2019).
8. Sir Ken Robinson, Do schools kill creativity?, 2006, Visit https://ted
.com and https://www.ted.com/talks/ken_robinson_says_schools_kill
_creativity#t-228488 (Accessed July 28, 2019).
9. https://www.artofmanliness.com/articles/the-35-greatest-speeches-in
-history/ (Accessed July 28, 2019).
10. http://www.emersonkent.com/speeches/the_third_philippic.htm
(Accessed July 28, 2019).
11. https://www.artofmanliness.com/first-inaugural-address-of-franklin-d
-roosevelt/ (Accessed July 28, 2019).
12. https://www.jfklibrary.org/learn/about-jfk/historic-speeches
/inaugural-address (Accessed October 16, 2019).
13. http://classics.mit.edu/Plato/apology.html (Accessed August 12, 2019).

Chapter 10: Once Upon a Time . . .

1. https://www.ncbi.nlm.nih.gov/pmc/articles/PMC2676782/ (Accessed
October 5, 2019).
2. Annu Rev Psychol. 2019 Jul 5. doi: 10.1146/annurev-psych-010419
-051123 (Accessed October 5, 2019).
3. https://www.ncbi.nlm.nih.gov/pubmed/28695528 (Accessed October
5, 2019).
4. https://wwl.radio.com/blogs/scoot/scoot-rolling-stones-don-t-act-their
-age 2. (Accessed August 20, 2019).
5. http://christopherwitt.com/stories/ (Accessed July 30, 2019).
6. https://visme.co/blog/7-storytelling-techniques-used-by-the-most
-inspiring-ted-presenters/ (Accessed October 22, 2019).

Chapter 11: Memorable Speeches of Yesteryear

1. Armanda Mabillard, *Why Study Shakespeare?* Shakespeare Online.
20 Aug. 2000. http://www.shakespeare-online.com/biography/
whystudyshakespeare.html (Accessed August 16, 2019).
2. The Complete Works of William Shakespeare, (New York: Crown
Publishers, Inc., 1975). The quotations of Shakespeare in the text not
listed in these Notes can be found online or in any complete collection of
his works.
3. William Shakespeare, *Henry V,* Act IV Scene iii 18-67 (The Complete
Works of William Shakespeare, (New York: Crown Publishers, Inc., 1975)
Also found at: http://poetrysociety.org.uk/poems/the-st-crispins-day
-speech-from-henry-v/ . (Accessed August 8, 2019).
4. William Shakespeare, *Julius Caesar,* Act III Scene ii 829-831. The
Complete Works of William Shakespeare, (New York: Crown Publishers,
Inc., 1975).

5. Brian Hooker, translation *Cyrano de Bergerac* by Edmond Rostand, (New York: Holt, Rinehart, & Winston, Inc. and Bantam Books, 1951).
6. http://forum.objectivismonline.com/index.php?/topic/1532-translations-of-cyrano/.
7. https://intrepidresources.com/assets/QMC.pdf (Accessed October 3, 2019).
8. See note 7 above.
9. *Wagner v. Int'l Ry. Co.*, 232 N.Y. 176, 133 N.E. 437 (N.Y. 1921).
10. Henry M. Boettinger, *Moving Mountains or The Art of Letting Others See Things Your Way*, (New York: Macmillan Publishing Co., Inc., 1969).

Chapter 12: Memorable Speeches in Times of Crisis

1. https://www.americanrhetoric.com/top100speechesall.html (Accessed October 5, 2019).
2. https://avalon.law.yale.edu/20th_century/mlk01.asp (Accessed October 5, 2019) and https://www.americanrhetoric.com/top100speechesall.html (Accessed October 5, 2019).
3. https://www.americanrhetoric.com/speeches/jfkinaugural.htm (Accessed October 5, 2019).
4. President Franklin Delano Roosevelt's First Inaugural Address https://www.bartleby.com/124/pres49.html (Accessed November 9, 2019).
5. https://www.americanrhetoric.com/speeches/fdrpearlharbor.htm (Accessed November 10, 2019).
6. https://www.fdrlibrary.org (Accessed August 17, 2019).
7. https://westpoint.edu/admissions/visit-west-point%20accessed%20August%2017 (Accessed August 17, 2019).
8. https://www.nationalww2museum.org (Accessed August 17, 2019).
9. https://www.nationalww2museum.org/visit/plan-your-visit/interactive-experiences/beyond-all-boundaries (Accessed August 17, 2019).
10. https://www.americanrhetoric.com/speeches/barbarajordan1976dnc.html (Accessed November 10, 2019).
11. https://www.americanrhetoric.com/speeches/ronaldreaganchallenger.htm (Accessed November 10, 2019).

Chapter 13: Memorable Speeches by Women

1. https://www.marieclaire.co.uk/entertainment/people/the-10-greatest-all-time-speeches-by-10-inspirational-women-79732#FMulLABZEvo0ymAF.99 (Accessed October 5, 2019).
2. https://en.wikipedia.org/wiki/A_Room_of_One%27s_Own (Accessed October 5, 2019).
3. https://conservativewomen.uk/content/pankhurst-freedom-or-death-speech accessed September 7, 2019).
4. Melinda Gates, *The Moment of Lift* (New York, Flatiron division of MacMillan, 2019).

5. https://www.ted.com/speakers/melinda_french_gates (Accessed October 5, 2019).
6. https://www.youtube.com/watch?v=8lztMXCdz0M (Accessed October 5, 2019).
7. https://www.gatesfoundation.org/Media-Center/Speeches/2007/10 /Melinda-French-Gates-Malaria-Forum (Accessed October 5, 2019).
8. https://allthatsinteresting.com/famous-speeches-by-women (Accessed October 5, 2019).
9. https://en.wikipedia.org/wiki/Malala_Yousafzai (Accessed October 5, 2019).
10. https://intrepidresources.com/djp_update/?p=1128.

Chapter 14: Memorable Speeches from the Web and Movies

1. https://www.youtube.com/watch?v=BxY_eJLBflk (Accessed September 1, 2019).
2. https://www.youtube.com/watch?v=UF8uR6Z6KLc (Accessed September 1, 2019).
3. https://www.fearlessmotivation.com/2018/06/06/bill-gates-inspiring -harvard-commencement-speech/ (Accessed Noveember 10, 2019).
4. https://news.harvard.edu/gazette/story/2007/06/remarks-of-bill-gates -harvard-commencement-2007/ (Accessed September 1, 2019).
5. (Donald J. Palmisano, *On Leadership* (New York: Skyhorse Publishing, 2008), 57.
6. https://www.youtube.com/watch?v=hzURem24MQU (Accessed November 19, 2019).
7. https://www.youtube.com/watch?v=utU9L8ONRbk (Accessed September 1, 2019).
8. https://en.wikipedia.org/wiki/The_Great_Dictator (Accessed September 1, 2019).
9. https://www.pri.org/stories/2014-12-19/what-we-can-learn-charlie -chaplin-and-great-dictator (Accessed September 1, 2019).

Chapter 15: TED Talks

1. https://www.ted.com/#/ and https://www.ted.com/participate/organize -a-local-tedx-event (Accessed July 31, 2019).
2. https://www.ted.com/playlists/171/the_most_popular_talks_of_all (Accessed July 31, 2019).
3. https://www.ted.com/talks/ken_robinson_says_schools_kill_creativity (Accessed October 19, 2019).
4. https://www.businessinsider.com/ted-talk-rules-for-presentations -2016-3 (Accessed July 31, 2019).
5. https://www.linkedin.com/pulse/20140313205730-5711504-the -science-behind-ted-s-18-minute-rule (Accessed July 31, 2019).

6.	https://creatoracademy.youtube.com/page/lesson/vlogging (Accessed November 10, 2019).
7.	https://www.copypress.com/blog/blogging-vs-vlogging-better / (Accessed November 10, 2019).
8.	https://www.vlognation.com/how-to-start-vlogging-youtube /(Accessed November 10, 2019).

Chapter 17: To Project or Not to Project . . . That Is the Question

1.	Cornell University article with images at http://www.birds.cornell.edu/ivory /evidence/segments/resultsunderwing (Accessed October 2, 2019).
2.	http://www.birds.cornell.edu/ivory/aboutibwo/studying_vanishing _html (Accessed October 2, 2019) and https://en.wikipedia.org/wiki /Ivory-billed_woodpecker (Accessed August 12, 2019).
3.	*Beyond Blame* video can be ordered at https://ismp.org/resources /beyond-blame.

Chapter 18: A Few Words about the Teleprompter

1.	https://www.realclearpolitics.com/lists/memorable_sotu/clinton_1994 .html (Accessed September 28, 2019).
2.	https://www.presidency.ucsb.edu/documents/address-before-joint -session-the-congress-the-state-the-union-12 (Accessed September 28, 2019).
3.	UPI reported in Los Angeles Times at https://www.latimes.com/archives /la-xpm-1985-05-08-mn-6375-story.html (Accessed September 28, 2019).

Chapter 20: Equipment for Practicing Speeches and Recording for Social Media

1.	Review of Sony recorder ICD-UX560 https://thewirecutter.com/reviews /the-best-voice-recorder/ (Accessed October 15, 2019) ICD-UX560.
2.	https://intrepidresources.com/djp_update/?cat=175 (Accessed November 2, 2019).
3.	https://www.youtube.com/user/curtisjudd/videos (Accessed November 2, 2019).

Chapter 21: Camera-Ready: Looking Your Personal Best

1.	Gerrie Pinckney and Marge Swenson, *Your New Image*, (Utah: Crown Summit Books, 1981).
2.	clothes/ (Accessed October 19, 2019).

Chapter 23: How to Get an Invitation to Speak

1.	https://www.barrypopik.com/index.php/new_york_city/entry/nothing _kills_a_bad_product_faster_than_good_advertising_advertising_adage (Accessed January 16, 2020).

INDEX